Receive One Another

Receive One Another
Hospitality in Ecumenical Perspective

Editor: Diane C. Kessler

WCC Publications, Geneva

Cover design: Marie Arnaud Snakkers
Cover picture: WCC/Peter Williams

ISBN 2-8254-1411-5

World Council of Churches
150 route de Ferney, P.O. Box 2100
1211 Geneva 2, Switzerland
Web site: http://www.wcc-coe.org

No. 110 in the Risk Book Series

Printed in Switzerland

Table of Contents

Preface

At first blush the phrase "ecumenical hospitality" seems something of a tautology. After all, would *inhospitable ecumenism* make any sense at all? If indeed we are concerned with promoting Christian unity throughout the world (which is *a* definition of ecumenism), should it not quite naturally follow that we would do our utmost to be welcoming and thoughtful towards those who are guests or strangers in our midst? While this sounds patently obvious, many of us who have been travelling the ecumenical road for a number of years can recall numerous occasions when we have at best found ourselves in an awkward position or at worst been offended by the insensitivity of other Christians from whom we expected better. These experiences do not create a fertile soil in which the tender plant of church unity can grow.

While books on the subject of ecumenism have been published in abundance, the concept of hospitality as a vehicle to enhance ecumenical progress has somehow stayed below the publishers' radar. The motivation behind the writing of this book is to make a modest effort to address this oversight.

The writers of this book intend to demonstrate that the mandate for hospitality, not only towards the stranger but also "especially to those who are of the household of faith" (Gal. 6:10 RSV), has its roots both in the Old and New Testaments. We will explore theological and historical foundations, as well as experiences in the area of ecumenical hospitality. We then shall offer some examples of what ecumenical hospitality looks like when practised well, and of some benefits gained in the quest for Christian unity. The concluding chapter of the book provides some resources, such as prayers, which may be used in the practice of ecumenical hospitality.

The contributors to this volume have been drawn from a broad cross-section of various Christian traditions, most of whom live in the greater Boston area of the United States; they include Protestants (mainline and evangelical), Anglicans, Roman Catholics and Eastern Orthodox. They come from academia, parish settings, as well as local and regional ecumenical organizations.

This book is not intended to be the last word on this subject, but the writing team hopes it will be a beginning attempt in what will become an ongoing conversation on this crucial topic. Christian unity is not just a pleasant avocation for the followers of Christ to dabble in at their leisure; it is the heart's desire of our Lord. Thus it follows that whatever we can do to promote and enhance our journey towards that unity is our urgent business because it is pleasing to our Lord.

George B. Elia
Convener, Ecumenical Hospitality Working Group

Introduction

In many parts of the world, ecclesial rites of passage – weddings, baptisms, funerals – increasingly involve Christians from different traditions. At these times of transition when families and friends are gathered together, Christian clergy and laity may find themselves either extending or receiving hospitality from a church of another tradition. When the experience is positive, it enables Christians to see the unity they share through Christ. Alas, sometimes the experience can be negative. When that happens, especially at such tender times, participants may leave with bitter memories not easily released.

Ecclesial events such as the installation of a new pastor or religious leader, or the ordination of a clergy-person or bishop, also are occasions when invitations are extended to representatives of other churches. These, too, may evoke strong feelings. If a delegation of clergy sit dutifully and respectfully through a two-and-a-half-hour service when a new religious leader and future colleague is being installed or ordained, but their presence is barely mentioned to the gathered congregation, they may wonder why they have bothered to give their time. If, on the other hand, not only are they thanked, but also their presence is interpreted as a visible sign of the real though incomplete communion we share through our baptism, those words will set a tone that enhances future relationships.

International travel to ecumenical events often elicits the strongest memories of ecumenical hospitality. A representative from Church World Service recently told the story of going to a village in Ghana. Upon his departure, he reluctantly received a gift of thirteen eggs in a woven basket. When he returned to his primary hosts in Accra, he was told that those eggs would be a full day's meal. His village hosts gave him all that they had. Such experiences leave indelible impressions.

Many people have journeyed for hours on several airplanes to get from their home to an ecumenical meeting being held in a country they have never visited before, where they do not speak the primary language. To be met at the airport with a welcoming smile from someone holding up a sign with their name on it may seem simple to the host, but it is an unforgettable gesture to the guest. Others have experienced arriving, travel-weary in an unfamiliar country late at night, being deposited by cab in what seems like a remote setting, standing at the door of an unfamiliar retreat centre, ringing a bell, and the door opening to a flood of light, an understanding smile, a fresh cup of tea, and a welcome room. Persons going from places of economic privilege to settings without similar resources often are struck by how people whose material possessions are modest are eager to display a courtesy, thoughtfulness and generosity of spirit that is humbling and inspiring.

This gift of abundant generosity is instructive for those people and cultures obsessed with time management and productivity. In these situations, the learning curve includes favouring personal relationships over agenda, accommodating unexpected and un-calendared events, and practising the sacrificial use of time, energy and resources for the sake of the invited guest or stranger at the gate.

These experiences among Christians are signs of ecumenical hospitality. They expand our appreciation for the ways we are called to love each other, to receive the ideas of the other and to stretch our understanding of the abundant nature of God's love.

Encounters like these led the board of directors of the Massachusetts Council of Churches (MCC) to authorize a project developing guidelines and good practices for the exercise of ecumenical hospitality. Initially the board members envisioned a project modest in scope and practical in application. They noted that it often has been the practice for a denomination or church to invite ecumenical guests to ecclesial events. The board noted that "the degree to which the full ecumenical significance of this practice is understood by host and guests has varied, as has the quality of hospitality extended. This situation presents an opportunity and a challenge."

One thing leads to another. Perhaps the Holy Spirit took this impulse and transformed it, because the project evolved into something far more ambitious, with potential ripple effects beyond what originally had been imagined. Several events combined to expand the project. When the World Council of Churches Faith and Order plenary commission met in Kuala Lumpur, Malaysia, in August 2004, the theme for the gathering was "Receive one another as Christ has received you for the glory of God" (Rom. 15:7). WCC general secretary Rev. Dr Samuel Kobia observed in his opening comments, "The Christian concept of hospitality may help the ecumenical movement to address the challenges of the 21st century with a sensitivity and creativity similar to those it showed when responding to major world crises during the previous century."

This Faith and Order focus coincided with an expression of interest in the project by the WCC Publications office. The Massachusetts Council of Churches was able to assemble a stellar drafting team of people who happen to live in the region, but who in many cases have had vast international ecumenical experience. We are deeply grateful for the time, interest and expertise they have given to this project. The drafting team also appreciated the ecumenical hospitality extended for our meetings by the Jesuit Residence of St Mary's Hall at Boston College, by Hellenic College/Holy Cross Greek Orthodox School of Theology, and by Andover Newton Theological School. These schools welcomed us warmly and provided tempting nourishment for our breaks.

So what started out as a pamphlet turned into a book. What began as simple guidelines developed into a potentially pioneering effort to take a fresh look at the biblical, historical, theological and spiritual foundations of the topic. Yes, the guidelines are here. But we also have looked at the roots and potential fruits of ecumenical hospitality.

Each of the participants brought unique gifts to the group, and the reader may detect distinct spiritual and ecclesial accents in different chapters. Nevertheless, the body worked as a team. The whole group reflected on each potential chapter before any drafting began. One individual with expertise in a particular area prepared a first draft after the whole group had reflected on the subject. That draft was reviewed with a consultant from a tradition different from that of the initial drafter; was considered by the whole group in what were lively dialogues; was revised in light of the discussion; and was refined in a final review. A general editor brought continuity to the text. The result is somewhere between a homogeneous "committee document" and chapters authored solely by a particular individual.

Because we were aware of the limitations of our predominantly North American context, we sent the penultimate draft to ecumenical colleagues in various parts of the world for comment. We are grateful for the insights of Rev. David Gill, Rev. Prof. Dr Viorel Ionita, Prof. Priscilla Lasmarias Kelso, Prof. Nicholas Lossky, Rev.

Fr Thomas Ryan CSP and Rev. Lydia Veliko. The text is stronger because of their help. Whatever inadequacies remain are the responsibility of the original drafting team, but we hope that this effort will stimulate further thought and action on this aspect of the churches' life together.

The group struggled to define "ecumenical hospitality". By the term "ecumenical", we mean initiatives to heal divisions among Christians and their churches for the sake of the world. By this definition, not all gatherings of Christians from different traditions necessarily are ecumenical. A *reconciling intention* is the ingredient that distinguishes between "ecumenical" and "interdenominational" situations. The Merriam-Webster dictionary defines "hospitable" as behaviour "given to generous and cordial reception of guests". Ecumenical hospitality, then, applies to generous and cordial actions between hosts and guests, which entail receiving persons in their wholeness – mind, body and spirit – by Christians and their churches, with an underlying or overt intention to heal the divisions among Christians for the sake of the world. This is, by definition, primarily a 20th and 21st century phenomenon, because ecumenical initiatives began to assume an ecclesial nature primarily in the last century.

The display of hospitality is not unique to Christians; nor is it confined to a particular era. Furthermore, as chapters two and three illustrate, Christians and their churches have offered hospitality from the beginning of the Christian experience. Furthermore, churches may engage in hospitable acts without a reconciling intention. All these are laudable expressions of kindness and generosity, but they are not the primary aim of this initiative. This book shines a lens on ways that expressions of hospitality, when given with thought and care by

Christians and their churches, can further the ecumenical quest for Christian unity.

We are aware that this definition and aim are self-limiting. Debates now are occurring among theologians and religious leaders about the basis on which Christians are engaged in interfaith relations. These debates were echoed in the drafting group. We recognize that fundamental questions for Christians about inter-religious relations are in flux and need to be addressed at the most authoritative level by the churches themselves. Thus, with some discomfort, the group decided to limit our attention to ecumenical issues, recognizing that many of the subjects raised may have wider application. We celebrate the intention to offer a text on inter-religious relations to attendees of the ninth assembly of the World Council of Churches from Faith and Order, the Commission on World Mission and Evangelism, and Inter-religious Relations and Dialogue, using the theme of hospitality.

The working group also has not addressed issues related to eucharistic[1] hospitality, other than to name the different perspectives churches hold on the issue, and to honour the pain that divisions among churches cause for Christians when the positions of churches rooted in faith convictions prevent eucharistic sharing. This issue also must be addressed by the churches themselves in official ecumenical relationships; but our drafting group joins the chorus of Christians who have experienced the remaining separations among churches most keenly at the eucharistic table, and who long for their resolution. And we spoke about those occasions when individuals were surprised with the joy of anticipatory acts borne of reconciling impulses that go beyond where the churches are able officially to venture.

We struggled with other issues during our gather-ings, as well. Periodically we found ourselves face to face with challenges the churches face in trying to deal with each other in love and truth concerning matters of gender inclusion and sexual orientation. We wrestled with language to define God. None of this is surprising, since these are ongoing challenges for churches together in the ecumenical movement. The group was perplexed about ways to honour concerns and sensitiv-ities. We agreed, for example, that while honouring the classic trinitarian language of "Father, Son and Holy Spirit", we wanted to demonstrate hospitality to those for whom this language is too confining by finding additional ways to name the Holy One. Because mem-bers of the working group come from different tradi-tions, this issue was handled in varied ways in different chapters.

In some contexts, churches are becoming increas-ingly introverted. The ecumenical impulse, which always has tended to be a minority movement in the life of the churches, is weakened to the degree that the churches themselves are struggling with internal chal-lenges. In such environments, matters of ecumenical hospitality may seem peripheral to more pressing con-cerns. Yet for those visionary and determined souls who honour the good practice of ecumenical hospitality and who support its implementation by the churches, they are "tilling the soil" (to use the image in chapter six) in readiness for the ecumenical impulse to grow. They really are at the heart of ecumenical formation and edu-cation.

Thus, the subjects raised in this book may be a good topic for dialogue among ecumenical governing bodies or gatherings such as ecumenical ministerial associa-tions. They could become "hand-books" for ecumenical officers and religious leaders. They may raise the awareness of parish clergy about the deeper reasons behind actions such as invitations to ecumenical colleagues that so often are taken for granted. All Christians, however, are called to "receive one another, just as Christ also received you, to God's glory" (Romans 15:7, New King James Version). The writers of this book hope – and yes, pray – that it will broaden and deepen the readers' appreciation of the promising potential that attention to ecumenical hospitality offers in the quest for Christian unity.

Diane C. Kessler
Editor

Ecumenical Hospitality Working Group*

Rev. George Elia, Convener
Evangelical Covenant
Church

Rev. Avedis Boynerian
Armenian Memorial
Congregational Church

Rev. Fr Francis J. Cloherty
Roman Catholic Church

Rev. Ian T. Douglas
The Episcopal Church

Ms Laura Everett
United Church of Christ

Dr Kyriaki Karidoyanes
FitzGerald
Ecumenical Patriarchate
(Greek Orthodox
Archdiocese of America)

Rev. Dr Thomas FitzGerald
Ecumenical Patriarchate
(Greek Orthodox
Archdiocese of America)

Rev. Dr Thomas A. Kane,
CSP
Roman Catholic Church

Rev. Renee K. Jackson
American Baptist Churches

Rev. Dr Richard McCall
Episcopal Church

Rev. Dr Elizabeth Nordbeck
United Church of Christ

Rev. Dr Edward O'Flaherty,
S.J. Roman Catholic
Church

Dr Simon B. Parker
United Methodist Church

Prof. Pheme Perkins
Roman Catholic Church

Rev. Karen L. Rucks
National Baptist
Convention, USA,
Inc./American Baptist
Churches, USA, Inc.

Bishop Krister Stendahl
Church of Sweden

Rev. Prof. George H. Tavard
Roman Catholic Church

Rev. Dr Diane C. Kessler,
Editor
Massachusetts Council of
Churches

*Churches are listed for purposes
of identification.

1. Hospitality in the Old Testament

The Old Testament does not, of course, envisage denominational ecumenism or inter-religious relationships. In fact, the opposite is often evident – hostility to and mockery of other religions, and hostility to religious groups in Judah other than that of the writers. So it is difficult to find warrants in the Old Testament for ecumenical hospitality. Nevertheless, there are passages that oppose the view of some religious groups that would exclude certain parties from full participation in their community. Instead, these passages announce the divine intention to welcome those who share a basic common commitment, even though they are held at a distance by others of the same faith.

Expressions of hospitality to the stranger and the treatment of resident aliens, however, are more prominent subjects in the Old Testament; so we will look initially at these broader topics, first through several stories that illustrate both the virtue of hospitality and its violation, and second through laws that call for beneficial treatment of immigrants and resident aliens.

Hospitality to the stranger

Hospitality to the stranger is a uniquely human trait. Strangers always are vulnerable and dependent on the friendliness of those among whom they pass or settle. In the ancient world, anyone might become such a stranger, driven from home by drought, warfare, famine or social marginalization. Perhaps that is why the practice of hospitality to strangers became a virtue. One offered, as one hoped to be offered, generous hospitality. Hence the Bedouin assurance, "you are among family", and a host of other assurances of welcome. The essence of hospitality is that it is freely given. While hoping that they would be treated similarly in similar circumstances, hosts did not expect to see the same strangers again.

In the guest-host relationship, the balance of power generally lies with the host who is among his own people. Genuine hospitality seeks to redress that imbalance. "The host is a little less at home and the guest, made to be at home, is a little less strange."[2] But the host, with no knowledge of the stranger or her background, also may feel vulnerable. Hospitality functions to neutralize the feelings of vulnerability in both parties. The host shows himself to be kind and generous, reassuring the guest; and the guest is put in a position of receiving benefits and so of being grateful, which reassures the host. Neither is any longer a threat to the other.

Yet hospitality still initially carries an element of risk or at least of anxiety. Both parties face unknowns. It is possible that one may be seen to be taking advantage of the other. It is possible to cause or experience insult without insult being intended.

In the ancient world, the risk of offence is minimized by certain universally accepted protocols. Three are illustrated in the Old Testament. In the first situation, the initiative lies with the host. The guest only can wait for an invitation, like the Ephraimite who enters the Benjaminite town of Gibeah at sundown, settles in the town square, and is ignored by all the townspeople until finally a fellow Ephraimite invites him into his home (Judg. 19:14-21). Ideally the guest does not have to wait. The host hastens to offer hospitality, as Abraham "runs" to the three strangers who appear near his tent (Gen. 18:2).

In the second situation, it is expected that the guest will leave after a day or two (cf. the proverb "houseguests and fish stink after three days"). Hence in the Bible, hosts have to be extraordinarily persuasive to prevail upon guests to stay more than the minimum time (Gen. 24:54-59), even when the two have a prior relationship (Judg. 19:4-10a).

In the third example, one may ask strangers where they are going and where they are from (Judg. 19:17), to establish whether they are far from home and therefore in need of hospitality; but hosts do not otherwise interrogate guests. It is left for guests to disclose as much as they wish about themselves. So Laban provides for the stranger's needs in Genesis 24 and asks nothing, even though in this unique case the stranger already has established a relationship with Rebecca and has sought the opportunity to follow up with her family. It is the stranger, Abraham's steward, who declines to touch the food set before him until he has introduced himself and recounted the history of his mission (see especially Gen. 24:31-33).[3]

Genesis 18:1b-8 and 19:1-3 depict hospitality to complete strangers. Genesis 18:1a begins, "Then Yahweh appeared to him..." This opening phrase tells the reader that Yahweh is coming to Abraham in the form of the three men, so the reader knows all along that Abraham is dealing with the deity. Abraham himself, however, simply sees, receives and entertains the three strangers. He has no idea who they are. Only later does he realize that this is a divine visitation. Thus, his hospitality is not offered especially for divine representatives, but simply for strangers who are passing by. Then in Genesis 18, Abraham and Sarah receive a blessing from God after the meal they have prepared. In ancient societies this was the possibility that reinforced hospitality. You never knew whether the stranger you were entertaining was a divine being (cf. the later New Testament reference to "entertaining angels unawares", Heb. 13:2). Such divine beings could be bearers of blessings or punishments (cf. the fates of Lot's family and of the inhabitants of Sodom in Genesis 19).

Although host and guest may enjoy a rewarding relationship, the neighbours of the host may object. In Genesis 19 and Judges 19 the hospitality offered by Lot and the Ephraimite is not shared by the other men of the town, who would violate the visitors. For various reasons, offering hospitality can give offence to one's neighbours. This Old Testament story reverberates in recent situations where, for example, people in an "Anglo" neighbourhood have reacted violently when one member of the neighbourhood has entertained people who looked different. Hospitality to outsiders is risky precisely because it treats the guest as an insider; other insiders may feel that their own identity is being threatened by the crossing of boundaries. To encourage hospitality it is necessary to expose the limiting effect of boundaries and to teach and demonstrate the liberating and rewarding effects of welcoming those who are different – a welcome based on deeper common commitments than those that divide.

Judges 19 takes this one step further by telling the story of an Ephraimite journeying from Bethlehem in Judah. As nightfall approaches, the Ephraimite comes to a non-Israelite city. His servant suggests that they spend the night there, but the man objects, preferring to stay in an Israelite town. In the story we read in Judges, the Israelite (specifically Benjaminite) town where they do spend the night is viciously inhospitable. The contrast is between those who are "other," who scarcely could have been less hospitable than the Israelite town, and those who are broadly related though of a different tribe. An analogy in our world might be an experience of hospitality extended by those of other religions in contrast with an experience of inhospitable behaviour by Christians towards each other. It would be a signal reproach to Christian churches if Christians found warmer hospitality from representatives of other religions than from other Christians.

Hospitality to the resident alien

The Old Testament has a lot to say about resident aliens, *gerim* – traditionally translated "sojourners" – people that, for whatever reason, had come from other places and settled temporarily or permanently in the local community. They may have been fleeing drought and famine in their own land, as Jacob's family did in the Joseph story, or injustice or warfare. Indeed, they may have settled in their new community for a variety of reasons. They not only may be of foreign origin – i.e. from other countries – but also from tribes other than one's own within Israel and Judah. In any case, the resident aliens now live among the native population. They are known personally by their new neighbours, but retain some distinctive customs and beliefs.

Gerim were welcome to participate fully in the religious life of the community – except for passover, for which circumcision of males was a prerequisite, as it was for all native Israelites (cf. the requirement of baptism for membership in the church). In this respect "there is one torah for the native and the resident alien" (Ex. 12:49). On the other hand, they were *required* to observe the sabbath.

How, then, should one treat the resident alien? The texts have some striking laws about the treatment of these "others". Leviticus 19:34 says, "You shall love [him] as you love yourself, for you were resident aliens in the land of Egypt." This law uses exactly the same wording as the command to love one's neighbour in verse 18. It is a distinctive expression – different from the usual way of expressing love of somebody (and attested otherwise only in 1 Kings 5:15 and 2 Chron. 19:2) – and probably means "to show love", that is, to express your love in concrete behaviour. Here in Leviticus 19, in a section of Leviticus now generally known as the "Holiness Code", the commandment to love one's neighbour has already been extended; the "neighbour" already has been reinterpreted centuries before the time of Jesus. The motivation for this law is the Israelites' own experience as aliens in Egypt. Similarly, in a law prohibiting mistreatment of *gerim*, Yahweh says, "For you know the life of the *ger*, for you were *gerim* in the land of Egypt" (Ex. 23:9).

Thus aliens are to be the objects of your love, just as your compatriots are, because you once were aliens yourself. The experience of being an outsider is the basis of showing hospitality to the outsider. Long before Jesus, then, the larger implications of the command to love one's neighbour were already being formulated, precisely in terms of the experience of being an alien – one who is not at home.

The Old Testament makes yet another use of the concept of the resident alien that is more generally theologically significant. While in some traditions Yahweh has given the Israelites their own land, in others they are described as guests on what is Yahweh's land: "The land is mine, you are aliens and tenants with me" (Lev. 25:23). Here all Israelites share the present experience of being resident aliens in the world in which God has placed them. In relation to God, the legally defined resident is no more alien than the native. This divine claim is especially significant for those of us who think of ourselves as *really* God's people and only of others as aliens! Instead, we are all aliens. We all need hospitality and we all need to be hospitable, for we are all aliens; and God, the lover of aliens, wants us to show such love to one another.

For Christians, the significance of the command to love one's neighbour has been sharply delineated once for all by Jesus. It is not just those with whom we get on well, not only the aliens who live peaceably among us, but even those with whom our community is at enmity. These, too, are to be the object of our care and hospitality. For Christians, hospitality to the neighbour includes the strangers among us and even those with whom we have been hostile.

Ecumenical hospitality, while it may involve individuals who are strangers, does not involve receiving people whose fundamental values and commitments are unknown, because we are speaking of people all of whom are in some way followers of Jesus as the Christ. Many people, however, are more aware of the distinctiveness of their own denomination than of the unity of the body of Christ. We function like resident aliens. "We" are God's home church and "you" other Christians are resident aliens. You live around us, but you are different. You are here on sufferance. (When one of the working group members lived in Kentucky in the early 1960s, he recalled that official forms asked for his "religion". The inquirers did not expect a response of Christian or Buddhist, however, but Baptist or Methodist, between which there evidently was a great divide!)

Hospitality to the religiously excluded

Finally, in more eschatologically oriented texts, some Old Testament prophecies see ancient Israelite sectarian divisions being overcome. Isaiah 56, for example, has been understood by some as the interpretive key to the whole last section of Isaiah, following the oracles of "Isaiah of Babylon" in chapters 40-55.

After a call to "practise what is just and do what is right" (vv.1-2) because of the imminence of God's deliverance, the prophet addresses two problematic situations: that of foreigners who have committed themselves to God but find that they are being excluded from God's people by the authorities who define such boundaries (v.3a); and that of eunuchs, who see themselves as having no future among God's people, here understood as having descendants to continue their line (v.3b). To the eunuchs God says that if they are keeping the sabbath and holding fast to the covenant, they will have a memorial in God's own house – an everlasting name that cannot be removed. In other words, God here assures people who have been judged as second-class members of the community that they will be represented permanently in the very house of God. They will not be marginalized, but always will be in God's presence at the centre of the people of God (vv.4-5). And to the foreigners – those who are led to believe that God excludes them from his people, even though they commit themselves to God, keep the sabbath and hold fast to the covenant – God gives a remarkable promise. God will lead them to the holy mount and give them cause for celebration in the holy house of prayer, so that it will be called "a house of prayer for all peoples". God's taking in of the faithful "other" transforms the very house of God from the protected territory of a particular group into a universally recognized and used sanctuary.

Both these situations send a tacit message to the religious authorities that are denying people full participation in the community: "You may exclude them, but God will place them at the centre of your life and will open his sanctuary (which you see as yours!) to all who confess God's name, so that it is recognized as a place of prayer for all of them." The final verse of this unit of text is to be interpreted in light of the argument of these verses: "I will gather yet others to those already gathered" (v.8). The in-group may have decided that it has included all those it has determined to be legitimate, but God is going to include others as well. Isaiah 66:18-21 envisages a similarly divine inclusiveness.

In the place of keeping sabbath and holding fast to the Mosaic covenant, Christians would place believing and living by the gospel, the new covenant. Like those eunuchs and worshippers of foreign origin excluded from full participation in the life of the worshipping community, however, Christians would do well to hear this judgment from Isaiah that discloses a divine point of view that is much more expansive than the narrow human rules by which we define our communities. Parochial as we are, we would do well to invite into our circles those whom God already has included.

It is the essence of ancient hospitality as practised in Israel to do for the stranger more than one normally does for one's own family – to offer the best. What a model for ecumenical hospitality – to honour the visitor more than one does one's own people!

2. Ecumenical Hospitality: New Testament Traces

A hermeneutical disclosure notice

In the fourth gospel, Jesus reassures his confused and troubled followers that his return to the glorious presence of God is a good thing. He has not given them a thick data-base to serve as technical support in the journey ahead. Instead, "When the Spirit of truth comes, he will guide you into all the truth; for he will not speak on his own, but will speak whatever he hears, and he will declare to you the things that are to come" (John 16:13).[4] In dealing with marriage questions posed by the Corinthians, St Paul distinguishes his discernment from the word of the Lord (1 Cor. 7:12). Such a determination is more than mere speculation or prudent legislation. The apostle concludes "I think that I too have the Spirit of God" (1 Corinthians 7:40).

Christians today face significant new questions. They bring to these questions insights from faith-filled lives that often have been nourished in more than one church. The openness to other Christians that many believers consider part of ordinary parish life is evidence of the success of the past century of ecumenism. Therefore ecumenical hospitality is as much a question for local churches as it is for more formal, official assemblies. Its most important elements – namely, the desire to encounter and get to know other believers precisely as different, and the acknowledgment that one's own faith will be nourished in the process – these insights are not advanced in the New Testament. "Hospitality" (Greek *philoxenia*; "hospitality to strangers", Heb. 13:2) for the first century audience indicated an openness to meet the other as a person in need, whether the stranger requiring food and shelter or the impoverished Christian sister or brother. Thus hospitality remained embedded in an asymmetrical pattern of social relationships connected with benefactors and their clients.[5]

Ecumenical hospitality requires that we encounter other believers as equal participants in a lived faith. Tensions between socio-cultural inequalities and the new equality of believers in Christ emerged as New Testament Christians assembled for the "Lord's supper".[6] Evidence for divisiveness in the earliest churches is analogous to the concerns of this study; both consider hospitality among those who share a common baptismal faith in Christ. Those instances in some ways are more analogous, however, to the tensions and splits within individual Christian churches than they are to our divided churches, since the inherited traditions, beliefs and practices of other believers reflected in the New Testament were not so foreign as to be a different religious association. In fact, there is little room for hospitality in the New Testament when the other represents a foreign deity. The first-century Christian communities are struggling to emerge as the distinctively other (true) faith in the context of Roman imperial order and its religious pluralism. Emphasis on establishing difference and boundaries was a necessary condition for the birth of Christianity.

Entertaining angels, receiving the stranger

In recommending the virtue of hospitality to its audience, Hebrews 13:2 evokes a familiar Jewish example (see the story of Abraham in Gen. 18:1-8), observing "... for by doing that some have entertained angels without knowing it". The Talmud invokes Genesis 18:3 in arguing that an obligation to show hospitality can override the rules for Sabbath rest (*b. Shab* 127a). The needs of the stranger are more pressing than this religious obligation to keep the sabbath. Religious zeal, even for the sabbath, must step back where hospitality is at stake.

The New Testament can perceive the divine presence hidden in the guise of visiting strangers as the risen Lord. The disciples on the road to Emmaus (Luke 24:13-35) press the stranger to remain with them because evening is approaching. Suddenly, the roles are switched. Jesus becomes the meal's host, engaging in the familiar eucharistic gestures of reclining, blessing and distributing bread to them (vv.28-31). The Emmaus disciples intended to host Jesus only to find him present as their host.

Elsewhere, Jesus' disciples, themselves, are stand-ins for their Lord. They are encouraged to rely on the hospitality and kindness of others as they go about the task of healing and bringing the message of God's rule (Matt. 10:40-42). God rewards even the simplest gesture of hospitality towards these "little ones". No change or conversion is being demanded of those who assist the disciples on mission. They can receive such hospitality, even acknowledge it as cooperation in realizing God's rule, with single-hearted gratitude. The disciples have no need for a pang of regret that their benefactor did not sign on with the Jesus team.

Perhaps even a bit of humility can be thrown into the mix. The churches are not always in the superior position as benefactors, the dispensers of hospitality. They are equally dependent upon the outsider who offers them hospitality.

Divided communities, differences between Christians

As Paul distilled nearly two decades of pastoral experience establishing churches in Asia Minor and Greece (Rom. 12:1-15:13), he addressed the question of hospitality among believers of diverse praxes. "Welcome those who are weak in faith, but not for the purpose of quarrelling over opinions," he writes (Rom. 14:1). From a broad cultural perspective, the danger of "quarrelling over opinions", especially among those who had drunk a bit too much, could ruin the conversation at any banquet symposium.[7] From the particular perspective of the Christian community, the sticking point lies in diversity of religious practice. The "strong" compared with the "weak in conviction" (Greek *pistis*) is a code for persons who will eat anything over against those who retain their Jewish heritage of keeping Kosher and religious holidays (14:5-6, 14). Though this distinction might appear to be simply one of Gentile or Jewish origin, Paul, a Jew, sides with the "strong"[8] and "the weak" might have included Christians of Gentile background who had adopted such Jewish customs.

The exhortation to "welcome one another" requires that these Christians of different persuasions receive one another into their homes or circle of friends. A church that only practises toleration at a distance cannot be said to practise Christian hospitality. The "strong" for whom food rules and holy days are what the ancient philosophers called "indifferent matters" *(adiaphora)* should act that way: receive the "weak" with the openness of Christ, not with thinly veiled feelings of superiority.

"Why do you pass judgment on your brother or sister? Or you, why do you despise your brother or sister?" (Rom. 14:10). Paul asks both sides to drop recriminations and acknowledge one another as faithful servants of the Lord (14:4). But it is not enough to do so at a distance. Since Christians are committed to seeking what builds up the body of Christ, they must interact with all of God's children: "Receive one another, therefore, just as Christ also has received you, for the glory of God" (Rom. 15:7 New King James Version).

If Romans provides general wisdom grounded in experience, earlier letters permit glimpses of how difficult the task could be in practice. Acrimonious words were exchanged between Paul and Peter in Antioch (Gal. 2:11-14). Paul admits that Peter willingly shared meal fellowship with non-Jewish believers. But he accuses Peter of hypocrisy for accommodating visitors from Jerusalem who were unwilling to do so. Is Peter not thereby just extending hospitality to guests? Barnabas and the others who joined Peter must have thought so.

Paul insists that such a division, even though a temporary arrangement, is not an indifferent matter. It undermines the baptismal equality of all believers represented in the formula of Galatians 3:28. It conveys a message that Christ has brought the non-Jews into a second-class relationship with God, a message Paul's Judaizing opponents in Galatia must have exploited. How often are ecumenical exchanges marred by such coded messages that the faith and practice of the other church is less faithful than it should be because it is not one's own?

If Romans 14 and Galatians 2 speak to religious divisions, 1 Corinthians 11:17-34 addresses socio-economic distinctions. The Corinthians were a fractious group. Almost every issue addressed involves factions or claims to superiority over other believers. Paul seeks metaphors of harmony, concord and communal solidarity to shift their perceptions of what it means to be in Christ. The most prominent metaphor depicts the church as Christ's body animated by the Holy Spirit.[9] Like the body, the church cannot survive without a single spirit guiding its activities and without a harmonious use of the diverse gifts of its members (1 Cor. 12:4-31).

The eucharistic formula that points to the shared bread as Christ's body (11:24) permits an identification between the shared loaf and the communal body. Questions of honour, patronage, relative wealth or status all turn up in the banquet culture of the ancient world. Houses with a formal dining room *(triclinium)* might accommodate only 9-12 persons in that area. Some authors suggest that dinners should be limited so that all can be served equal portions of food and can share in the conversation that follows.[10]

The exact order of events in 1 Corinthians 11:17-34 is unclear. However, one group evidently has plenty to eat and drink while another suffers the humiliation of having nothing (11:21-22). Perhaps a wealthy host and his friends are feasting in the *triclinium*, while the poorer Christians are assembled in the atrium, waiting for the ritual bread and wine to be distributed. Whatever the details, Paul's assessment of the situation is clear. The "body of Christ" constituted by those assembled must be respected. That respect requires that every person be treated equally. Paul tells those who are stuffing themselves to eat at home before they leave for the meeting (vv.22a,34). The Lord's supper does not require lavish banqueting. It does require that each person be received as Christ. Paul backs up his injunction with a warning that disdain for Christ's body could be correlated with other ills being experienced in the community (vv.27-32).

Discrimination in the Christian assembly surfaces in James 2:1-13 as well. The wealthy individual is accorded a place of honour, the poor told to sit at someone's feet or to stand. The author castigates the audience for not holding the "faith of our glorious Lord, Jesus Christ" (2:1)[11] because the assembly engages in such partiality towards the rich. Cultural habits of deference to wealthy patrons die hard. Though they know something of God's "preferential option for the poor" (v.5) and have suffered abuse at the hands of the rich (vv.6b-7), Christians continue to act like their neighbours, not like the Lord.

James follows the specific case with a general warning to see to it that deeds and words match, that mercy prevails (vv.12-13). Those who engage in discrimination are guilty of breaking the "royal law", love of neighbour (vv.8-9). This example points to the importance of ecumenical hospitality in routine parish life. What reception does the ordinary visitor from a different Christian tradition receive when she or he comes into the church alone or as the guest of church members?

Barriers to hospitality

As Hebrews 13:2 indicates, hospitality regularly appears as a virtue that is enjoined upon Christian congregations (see also Rom. 12:13; 1 Pet. 4:9). In the pastoral epistles, hospitality is one of the virtues required of those who have charge of local communities (1 Tim. 3:2; Tit. 1:8). Hospitality is closely linked with love of neighbour as James 2:8-9 and Romans 12:13 suggest, since it involves meeting the needs of others.

Genuine hospitality fails when other concerns or social habits distort one's sense of what it means to receive the outsider as Christ. A more troubling situation emerges when other Christians are not to be received on principle. The Johannine epistles provide a case in point. Second John 10-11 requires a doctrinal testing of those to be received. Anyone suspected of dissident teaching must not be received: "Do not receive into the house or welcome anyone who comes to you and does not bring this teaching, for to welcome is to participate in the evil deeds of such a person." In 3 John, the elder must seek hospitality for his associates from the addressee, Gaius, because another prominent Christian in the same region refused them hospitality. One cannot be certain of the motive for that denial. Perhaps the elder is being given a dose of his own medicine.

Didache 11:4-12:2 collects a number of practical rules for communities to use in receiving and evaluating wandering prophets. Though evaluation of the prophet's teaching by received teaching has a role (11:11), the primary concerns are economic. The true prophet will stay only one or two days and ask for what is necessary to sustain life.

Though these barriers to hospitality may have been fairly low at the end of the first and early second century, both doctrinal disagreements and more pragmatic rules of exclusion would continue to separate Christians. Hospitality is being denied because taking in such persons threatens inherited beliefs or practice. Consequently, the one who is excluded remains unknown, or worse, demonized. Ecumenical hospitality is needed to heal the wounds that the body of Christ has suffered as a result of centuries of division.

Eating with dubious companions, Jesus at table

The gospels repeatedly depict Jesus associating with the marginalized, revenue collectors and others lumped in the category of "wicked". Such behaviour was grist for the mill of those who challenged Jesus' claim to speak God's word. As the conclusion to the parable of children playing in the market place has it: "For John the Baptist has come eating no bread and drinking no wine, and you say, 'He has a demon'; the Son of Man has come eating and drinking, and you say, 'Look, a glutton and a drunkard, a friend of tax collectors and sinners!' Nevertheless, wisdom is vindicated by all her children." (Luke 7:33-35).

Luke repeatedly employs the scenario of meal hospitality to show Jesus drawing such persons into the new fellowship representing God's reign (e.g. Luke 19:1-10). However, Luke also paints the Pharisees, even those who host Jesus, as emblematic of greed, of hostility towards the sinner or of fellowship denied (Luke 11:37-44, 14:1-14).[12] He has relocated the story of a woman anointing Jesus from its traditional place in the Passion narrative (Mark 14:3-9, at the house of Simon the leper) to a dinner hosted by Simon, the Pharisee (Luke 7:36-50). Jesus responds to Simon's unvoiced thought that he must know what sort of woman she is; a teacher would not permit a sinner to touch him. The verbal exchange between them includes a sharp attack on Simon's lack of hospitality: "I entered your house; you gave me no water for my feet[13] but she has bathed my feet with her tears... You gave me no kiss, but from the time I came in she has not stopped kissing... You did not anoint my head with oil, but she has anointed my feet. Therefore, I tell you, her sins, which were many, have been forgiven; hence[14] she has shown great love. But the one to whom little is forgiven, loves little" (Luke 7:44-47).

These comments show that the story is not about hospitality in any culturally defined sense of *quid pro quo*. It is not about showing appropriate respect to an honoured guest. The woman's gestures are expressions of "great love", not protocol.[15] Something about the excessive self-forgetfulness of love is suggested by this story. The woman has gone far out of her way to find the Lord – even into a Pharisee's house where she clearly is not welcome – and may even have spent all that she had. Hospitality will go the extra mile to embrace another in love.

Concluding reflections

Ecumenical hospitality in the spirit of the Lord may risk such excesses of love. Fears that the stranger will bring some form of doctrinal or moral infection into the pious household of faith can be acknowledged. Simon silently accused Jesus of not knowing what sort of woman the intruder was. Jesus knows both Simon and the woman better than they know themselves. He exposes where they stand in that all-important criterion, love of neighbour and of God. In part, that is also the risk of ecumenical hospitality. To come to know and receive each other in faith will expose the failures and weaknesses of division. It will uncover the subtle and not so subtle ways that those of other faith traditions find themselves assigned to inferior spots at the table.

Hospitality in the New Testament concerned meeting the need of the other without locking the recipient into the subordination to wealth and power that the patron-client system demanded. Ecumenical hospitality addresses new questions that have emerged from the ecumenical experiences of the 20th century. How can believers welcome and come to know one another on the deep level that love requires?

3. Hospitality: Insights from Our Common Heritage

The contemporary ecumenical movement seeks to heal divisions of the churches and restore their unity so that God will be glorified and the gospel will be proclaimed more faithfully. Beginning in the late 19th century, this movement has been characterized by prayers for reconciliation, by theological dialogue and by common witness in society. Through these expressions, the followers of Christ from divided churches have had opportunities to meet one another in an atmosphere of mutual respect and love. They have had occasions to offer hospitality to one another and to receive hospitality from one another in Christ's name.

The ecumenical movement also can provide occasions to look together at those expressions of hospitality that are part of our common Christian heritage. These historic expressions can provide insights into the importance of "ecumenical hospitality" in the quest for reconciliation and unity.

A monastic tradition

The early monastic tradition placed particular emphasis on the virtue of hospitality for visitors. Monasteries were primarily communities of monastics whose lives centred upon regular prayer offered for the church and for the world. At the same time, monasteries often were the destination of pilgrims who sought spiritual nourishment or guidance. They also were a safe place of rest for weary travellers.

In his rule for monastic communities, St Benedict of Nursia (c.480-c.547) paid particular attention to the importance of hospitality. He directed that pilgrims and travellers be welcomed and honoured by the monastery. In this expression of hospitality, the monastics bore witness to the gospel in a very practical way. To the monks, Benedict said, "All guests who present themselves are to be welcomed as Christ. Great care and concern are to be shown in receiving poor people and pilgrims, because in them more particularly is Christ received." Affirming the relationship between Christ and the guest, St Benedict said, "All humility should be shown in addressing a guest. Christ is to be adored in them because he is indeed welcomed in them" (Rule, 53).

As part of the ecumenical movement, many monasteries and retreat centres of different churches and traditions have related the virtue of hospitality to the quest for reconciliation and unity. These communities have welcomed believers from various Christian churches and traditions who seek a place for prayer, retreat, fellowship and spiritual growth. Often these centres, such as the famous community of Taizé in France, have become significant communities of hospitality.

Pilgrimages

Especially after the end of persecutions in the 4th century, Christian pilgrims began to undertake journeys to significant places associated with the life of Christ as well as with Mary, the apostles and other early saints. Jerusalem and other towns in the holy land were among the pre-eminent destinations of pilgrims. As time went on, other important places also attracted pilgrims from throughout Europe. Among these were Rome, Constantinople, Santiago de Compostela and Canterbury. In these places, pilgrims came to pray in the churches and to venerate the relics of holy women and men.

These pilgrimages also provided the opportunity for encounters between believers from different places and cultures. As they travelled, pilgrims received the hospitality of local believers who offered not only encouragement and support but also a place to eat and to rest. Pilgrims certainly could not undertake their journeys without the hospitality of fellow believers at various places along their route. Those who offered hospitality to pilgrims made the journey possible and shared in its blessing.

As part of the ecumenical movement, a new expression of pilgrimage has highlighted the concern for reconciliation and church unity. These pilgrimages bring together believers from different churches and, often, from different cultures. Like their historic predecessors, these "ecumenical pilgrims" frequently journey together to the holy land and to other places rich in Christian significance. The journey provides the pilgrims with an opportunity to experience different expressions of church life and worship. The pilgrimage nurtures a greater sense of the breadth and depth of the Christian experience. The journey also is a unique occasion for prayer and reflection together. As an important part of their pilgrimage, participants experience the hospitality of other believers who welcome the pilgrims.

Councils

In the post-apostolic period, the practice of gathering in council (synod) became firmly established. These councils normally brought together bishops and other church leaders from throughout a particular geographical region. The bishop was the principal leader of a local church, eventually known as a diocese. At the same time, the bishop also was a sign of the unity of faith and communion among the local churches. Councils provided the opportunity for the bishops to meet and, when necessary, to elect new bishops. Thus, the celebration of the holy eucharist by the bishops in council became the foremost expression of unity.

In the face of heretical teachings, the councils also were occasions when theological challenges could be

discussed and the apostolic faith affirmed. In their decisions, the councils sought to strengthen the unity of the
churches, and to restore that unity when it was broken.
Certainly not all the councils, local or regional,
achieved their goal, but each council took inspiration
from the council of apostles described in Acts 15.
Among the conciliar gatherings, the so-called "ecumenical councils" of the early church, together with
their specific challenges, are better known. Yet these
councils reflected the deeper conciliar tradition that was
essential to the life of the church.

The councils also were important events at which
hospitality was expressed. Although the gatherings took
place in a particular city, most of the participants came
from surrounding cities and towns. Indeed, the ecumenical councils brought together participants from
regions throughout the Roman-Byzantine empire.
While the participants believed that they were part of
the one church of Jesus Christ, they gathered together
with their cultural and linguistic differences. The
bishop and faithful of the local church were those who
provided hospitality for the visitors who came for the
council. They were the hosts who welcomed church
leaders and faithful from far and wide.

The ecumenical movement has recognized the critical
need for representatives of separated churches and ecclesial communities to engage in theological dialogue
within the context of prayer and mutual respect. Mindful
of the councils of the early church, numerous ecumenical conferences and dialogues have provided the occasion to examine points of theological difference and to
propose resolutions that can contribute to reconciliation.

These meetings have been enriched greatly by the
hospitality of the local Christian community. As part of
the gatherings, parishes of different traditions have

hosted visitors from neighbouring towns and from distant lands. The faithful have welcomed visitors into their worship services and into their homes. They have shared their stories of faith and expressed their hope for reconciliation. New relationships have been established, and these have challenged the old pattern of divisions.

Communities of care

In the middle of the 4th century, St Basil the Great (329-379), the bishop of Caesarea in Cappadocia, Asia Minor, was renowned as a loving pastor and thoughtful theologian. At the same time, he was also known for his compassion and care for those in need. With remarkable devotion and foresight, Basil established a community of care, known as the *Basileias*. Centred around a beautiful church, this village included a hospital, a home for the poor, a home for the elderly, an orphanage and a home for lepers. Residences were provided for the staff of clergy, doctors, nurses and other care-givers. Hospitality also was provided for visiting relatives, clergy and government officials. Basil himself frequently visited the sick, poor and outcast who lived in this special community of care. He directed that hospitality and care be offered to all those in need regardless of their religious convictions or cultural backgrounds. Speaking of the care for those in need, he wrote, "The goal which everyone ought to have in their work is to help the needy, more than to provide for oneself. In this way, we shall avoid the accusation that we are attached to our own personal advantage and we shall receive the blessing that the Lord gives to those who love their brothers and sisters" (The Great Rules, 42).

Basil's community provided the inspiration for countless hospitals, hospices, orphanages, as well as homes for the poor and the elderly that could be found throughout the Byzantine empire from the 4th to the 15th century. Supported both by church and government, these communities of care for the needy influenced similar institutions that subsequently developed in Western Europe.

As part of the ecumenical movement, many Christians from different churches and traditions have affirmed their obligation to work together to assist those in need. Hospitals, orphanages and homes for the needy, originally often established by particular churches to serve their own, now have opened their doors to all. In many places, parishes of different traditions also have come together to provide services such as food distribution, counselling and health care. Challenging old patterns of division, hospitality and care for the needy are being extended to all in Christ's name.

ory of the group. This, in turn, contributes to shaping the future of the church and of the churches together.

Some historical background through a particular lens

One of the most spectacular instances of ecumenical hospitality in recent memory happened when Pope John XXIII invited the Eastern Orthodox, Oriental Orthodox, Anglican and Protestant churches to send observers to the sessions of Vatican Council II (1962-65). Sending invitations was not exactly new in 1962. In the 16th century Protestants were invited to the council of Trent. They did not attend, presumably because they remembered the fate of John Hus, who in 1415, having come to the council of Constance under the protection of an imperial safe-conduct, was nevertheless burnt at the stake for alleged heresy. In 1869 Orthodox bishops were invited to Vatican Council I. Distrustful of the bishop of Rome for long-standing historical and doctrinal reasons, however, they abstained from attending. Pius IX's known interest in a definition of papal infallibility evidently was not attractive to them. Whatever concerns were in the mind of Pius IX when he faced what he regarded as a hostile world, the promotion of ecumenical relations was not among them. The situation began to shift with his successor Leo XIII, whose conception of "unionism" (encyclical *Satis Cognitum*, 20 June 1896) at least intended to foster the unity of Christians, even though his view of the Reformation led him, through the condemnation of Anglican ordinations (apostolic letter *Apostolicae Curae*, 13 September 1896), to place a high hurdle along the way of reconciliation. What was totally new in the invitations sent by John XXIII was their explicitly ecumenical intent.

Accepting ecumenical invitations was, likewise, not new. The primary examples thus far had been set, not by a church, but by the leading personalities of the Faith and Order and the Life and Work movements, who were able to introduce a new concern for Christian unity in their churches. In 1919 and 1921, however, Pope Benedict XV declined invitations to send Catholic participants to the projected assemblies. Nevertheless, some progress was made when, in 1921, he looked with sympathy on Cardinal Mercier's sponsorship of the unofficial Malines conversations between Anglican and Catholic theologians. His successor Pius XI continued to encourage Cardinal Mercier, at whose death in 1925 the conversations came to an end. Pius XI, however, remained generally negative when he judged that the Faith and Order and Life and Work movements were promoting "pan-Protestantism" (encyclical *Mortalium Animos,* 6 January 1928). In contrast, in the holy office instruction *Ecclesia Catholica* (20 September 1949), Pius XII recognized the ecumenical movement as prompted by the Holy Spirit, and he affirmed the local bishop's authority to authorize Catholic participation in ecumenical gatherings in each diocese. No official Catholic observer attended the creation of the World Council of Churches (WCC) in 1948, but observers were invited and sent to the Faith and Order meetings of Lund (1952) and Oberlin (1958), as well as to the central committee of the WCC meeting in Nyborg (Norway) in 1958. Not all bishops, however, responded positively to ecumenical invitations. In 1954, Cardinal Samuel Stritch, archbishop of Chicago, explicitly forbade Catholics from attending the second assembly of the WCC in Evanston.

When the Pontifical Secretariat for Promoting the Unity of Christians was created by John XXIII in 1960, ecumenical hospitality during the Vatican council became one of its responsibilities. Reciprocity soon followed, showing that there was a general desire for better mutual knowledge among the churches. In 1961 Catholic observers attended the third assembly of the World Council of Churches in New Delhi. In 1963 five official Catholic observers attended the Faith and Order meeting in Montreal.

Ecumenical hospitality, theologically defined

Ecumenical hospitality can henceforth be described as a church-to-church relationship in which invitations are extended and accepted. The task of defining it theologically in the context of the church ought to proceed at several levels. The most obvious aspect derives from its basis in ecumenical dialogue. While the following passage from the decree on ecumenism of Vatican Council II approaches dialogue from a Catholic angle, it can speak for all Christian traditions:

> It is necessary that Catholics joyfully acknowledge and esteem the truly Christian goods, coming from a common heritage, that are found among the brothers separated from us. It is right and salutary to acknowledge the riches of Christ and the virtuous works in the lives of others who bear witness to Christ, sometimes to the shedding of blood: God is always admirable and should be admired in his works.
> And one should not omit that whatever is done in our estranged brothers by the grace of the Holy Spirit can also contribute to our own upbuilding. (*Unitatis redintegratio,* n.4).

All Christian believers ought to nurture relationships with members of churches other than their own, in the dimensions of both offer and acceptance, that may contribute to the mutual edification and spiritual emulation of all. Desire for the unity of Christians resonates as an echo of the prayer of Jesus "that all may be one..." (John 17:21). Desire should inspire action. This presupposes better mutual knowledge. Knowledge, however, does not by itself effect changes of attitude. Change involves a process of "interior conversion" and "renewal of heart" (UR, n.7), as when individuals and communities turn away from self-centredness to other-centredness. This cannot be done by virtue of human intention and effort alone. The Holy Spirit, working by divine grace in the Christian soul, enables believers and their communities to cherish other Christians as themselves.

The proper locus of ecumenical hospitality is not individual believers. It is the churches themselves. Even though such hospitality may require personal conversion on the part of church leaders and of the faithful, it is not their achievement. It may flow from their initiatives and be nurtured by their encouragement. Yet ecumenical hospitality requires a corporate mindset in the teachings and practices of the churches themselves.

The structure of all churches ought to be radically dialogical. A church is necessarily in dialogue with itself, with other Christian believers, and with the world in both its secular and its religious dimensions. While this insight lay at the heart of Paul VI's first encyclical letter (*Ecclesiam Suam*, 1963), it had been a basic principle of the World Council of Churches since its beginnings in 1948.

In its secular dimension, the world questions and challenges the church. The church, in turn, listens to the world. In doing so, the church learns from scientific discoveries and the sharing of information, from the aspirations to universal peace that are expressed in literature and in the arts, from the emergence and development of systems of law, from progress towards equity and justice in the organization of society. The church also learns by reflection on the mistakes that are made in the difficult process of offering respectful service to humanity so indispensable to life in a peaceful society. To this world and its inhabitants the church strives to bring the gospel as a force of spiritual and social liberation.

In its religious dimension the world gives examples of the search for ultimate values and offers ways to depict and worship God among those who are in ignorance of the gospel of Christ. The many religions that have grown outside of the Judeo-Christian context orient men and women to God in many diverse ways. This orientation of humankind towards a supreme principle, who dwells within and presides over all that is, sets the contexts and conditions in which the gospel needs to be announced, thus helping to shape the churches' conception and practice of mission.

Catholicity – the theological foundation of ecumenical hospitality

It is hardly accidental that the very word "ecumenical" derives from the Greek term *oikumene*, the meaning of which is closely related to "universal" and "catholic". Since the great prophets called the people of Israel, as people of God, to act as the one pole of attraction for the whole of humanity in search of God, this universal orientation became one of the fundamental marks of the Christian church. The theological locus of ecumenical hospitality lies in the catholicity that the creed of Nicaea-Constantinople ascribes to the church. The church is "one, holy, catholic and apostolic". These marks or qualities are not goals that can be reached by human effort. They are, first, gifts of the Spirit to the community of true believers and, second, ideals to which the faithful in all their groupings ought to turn in their thoughts and actions. Each mark points to an aspect of the Christian way of life: unity of love, holiness of worship and life, catholicity of concern and commitment, apostolicity of tradition and teaching. As the four marks together determine the actual shape of the church, each one of them implies an obligation, an ideal to be pursued, which has both a corporate and a personal dimension.

At the corporate level, catholicity (deriving from the Greek *kath olon*, "in keeping with the whole") has its focus in the potential universality of the church on earth. This universality is grounded in God's offer of salvation through Jesus Christ to all women and men without exception. In individual Christians it takes the form of a total commitment of soul and body to God and the neighbour. In the church as communion it is expressed in intent and it nurtures mission. It inspires the intention to be faithful to the totality of the commission received from Christ, including the mission to preach the gospel to all nations. While catholicity is not primarily geographic, the universality of the Christian faith on earth builds up slowly through the ages as the gospel is proclaimed and received in more and more lands. Worldwide universality mirrors a more interior and spiritual universality that ought to inspire the commitment of the faithful to make themselves neighbours to all women and men. This ought to be incorporated in the teaching and practice of Christian ethics. It is to be progressively achieved in the course of human history, so that it should eventually embrace all inhabited lands and transform all dimensions of culture.

Such openness to the universal is not a human work. The desire of it derives from the Spirit, who also enables the faithful and their communities to reach out to others in acceptance and love. Among individuals it requires a personal opening of the believers' heart and soul to the universal dimension of God's love and compassion for all creatures. Among Christian communities it must contribute to modelling all structure and life on God's universal purpose for creation and humankind.

In the history of Christianity, catholicity has taken the form of *koinonia* (communion) in the common prayer and the common life of local churches and in their solidarity in the universal church, of conciliarity or synodality *(sobornost)* in provincial, regional and ecumenical councils, and of collegiality in the responsibility and concern of bishops and leaders for all the churches. It is manifested in solicitude and care for the known and unknown sisters and brothers in Christ who live beyond the limits of one's local church, as also for those persons all over the world who have not been reached by the gospel in their life and commitment. Such solicitude and care ought to shape the prayer and the actions of individual believers.

In the conditions of fragmented Christendom catholicity has, at least since the missionary conference of Edinburgh in 1910, taken new institutional forms that have helped to stretch the imagination of Christians everywhere, so that the unity of the disciples for which Jesus prayed can reasonably be considered a realizable goal for which to strive. Thus new forms of concerns and relations beyond the limits of each church are now at work in the missionary endeavours of churches to preach the gospel through the whole world.

Baptism widens the horizons of Christians

Catholicity is not an abstraction, and it does not exist in a vacuum. It is profoundly inscribed in the structure of Christian life by virtue of its connection with baptism. This sacrament, which is common to most churches though with different theological emphases, has traditionally been known as the first sacrament of Christian initiation. The differences in the understanding of baptism that exist between theologies and churches do not affect a fundamental consensus, as was explained in the Faith and Order paper *Baptism, Eucharist and Ministry* (1982). Baptism is so closely tied to the gift of faith that it is seen as the introduction of believers into the Christian life. Whether it is understood as the sacrament through which faith is infused by the Spirit, or as a public recognition that faith has effectively been given and received, baptism marks the believer's entry into the Christian church. This is independent of the particular accents that different theologies have placed on its connection with other sacraments or Christian ordinances, or on its implications for Christian life and ethics.

Properly speaking, baptism does not identify members of the denomination in which it has been received, but rather members of the universal church of Christ. Because it is not a private action, but an event in which a community acts as both context and witness of the Spirit's action, it sets the baptized person on the horizon of the entire community in which the spiritual goods associated with baptism are shared. It establishes all Christian believers in a relationship of communion, of being and belonging together, whatever superficial differences separate them. Such a sharing should eventually take the form of common witness and common mission. In principle, therefore, baptism opens the baptized to all the others who also have been baptized, so that they together may witness to the One by whom they are justified and in whom they believe, the Word incarnate Jesus Christ. Whether it is so acknowledged or not, this witness echoes the traditional creeds formu-

36

lated in the ecumenical councils of the first centuries. Since the spiritual roots of each Christian reach far into the past in the creeds and the scriptures, they constitute a strand in the chain of transmission that is the Christian tradition. Like the faith itself that is transmitted, they are formative of God's future on earth until the final manifestation of the glory of Christ.

Challenges remain

It would seem logical that the common baptism of Christians should lead to a common eucharist. By its very nature as the first sacrament of Christian initiation, baptism, the sacrament of participation in the dying and rising of Christ, calls for the eucharist, the sacrament of participation in so close a discipleship that it includes the presence of Christ in and among his disciples. This is, however, where the tragedy of Christian divisions is so sharp that, at least for Orthodox and Catholic churches, it cannot at this time be overcome by a desire for ecumenical hospitality. Because these churches see an intimate connection between ecclesial communion and eucharistic communion, they cannot consent to full eucharistic hospitality without drastic structural conversions in all churches. That the eucharist is a meal in which the Lord is at the same time host and food may well justify a prophetic stance of eucharistic hospitality by individual believers in their own specific circumstances. But this is hardly sufficient to overcome convictions of faith in regard to the nature and structure of the church in such a way that universal eucharistic hospitality can soon become a common Christian experience.

The breaks of communion between Roman Catholic and Orthodox churches and the churches of the Reformation brought a great deal of disarray into the process of hospitality. Nonetheless, the churches and their members are so profoundly rooted in faith and baptism that they remain in communion, though in a partial, incomplete or imperfect way. This is the most fundamental grounding of ecumenical hospitality. Inviting other communities into one's own church's life and witness is one way to keep a degree of contact at the official level, and to share or, where needed, to recover the sense and the reality of mutual responsibility for one another.

Moreover, through faith and baptism the Holy Spirit inspires many believers to entertain at least an implicit desire to nurture closer ties, not only with all Christian believers, but also with the many women and men who worship God in other religions, and who seek the ultimate meaning of their life in a relationship with the transcendent Principle of all that is and that will be.

Faith opens the heart and mind

What has been said of baptism as a defining Christian action applies equally to the faith to which baptism testifies. Faith opens the heart and mind to the full scope of God's purpose in creation and in the incarnation, whether it precedes a sacramental action and inspires an adult to ask for baptism in a Christian community, or it is infused in baptism as a divine gift that should unfold progressively in one's conscience and transform one's life according to the gospel. Since God's purpose includes the conversion of the nations to the covenantal relationship with God that is described in the Bible, the faith expressed in baptism implies a call to minister to others, and to take part in the apostles' mission to make disciples of all nations (Matt. 28:18).

Whether the primary fruit of faith is identified as the justification by God of a sinful person, or as the insertion of the baptized in the God-given community of believers, faith is not a belief in oneself, but in God and in God's promises and gifts. It is not a tool that can be appropriated, but a signpost leading to the believers' commitment in love to all those who are embraced in God's salvific intent manifested through Jesus Christ. It has a dimension of involvement, both in the general human community to make it more fraternal, just and compassionate, and in the community of the faithful, the church, to make it a more effective witness to the gospel. Ecumenical hospitality is a way for a Christian community to acknowledge its communion of faith with other Christian communities. This communion extends back in time to the first disciples of Jesus and to the church through the ages. It extends in space across the borders of tribes, nations and continents. It should also extend, in ecumenical friendship, across the dividing lines of Christian institutions and denominations.

Making room for others in imitation of the divine life

Baptism traditionally is conferred "in the name of the Father and of the Son and of the Holy Spirit". Faith primarily is directed towards the First Person, as in the traditional creeds. After professing faith in God, the Father almighty, the creeds go on to profess faith in the Word of God who took flesh for our salvation, and in the Holy Spirit. In the theological controversies of the 5th and 6th centuries it became clear that the whole movement of faith ascends to the First Person "through" Christ, the only Mediator, "in" the grace of the Holy Spirit. In the 16th century the Reformers rightly insisted that the saving design of God, manifested in the justification of the sinner, reaches the latter through the actions and merits of the Word made flesh, Jesus Christ, and is effective through the power of the Spirit. Thus the believers' relation with Christ has its source and its model in the Holy Trinity. The trinitarian scope of baptism and of faith leads the faithful to see the pattern of their life in the Holy Trinity itself. This is true of the church as a communion no less than of the faithful as individual persons.

The doctrine of the Trinity includes what the Greek tradition calls the *perichoresis*, and the Latin tradition the "circumincession", of the three divine Persons. These terms are intended to mean that the relations between the Father, the Word and the Spirit are not static. The Persons do not simply stand facing one another in what, in 1439, the council of Florence called an "opposition of relations" (*DS* 1330). They also move into one another in a motion that implies neither the passage of time nor the crossing of space. They dwell in one another without, however, ever being limited by location.[16]

As in everything else, human persons and institutions only can imitate the divine life imperfectly in their mutual relations. They nevertheless truly imitate God when they try to make room in themselves for the concerns of others, to rejoice in the achievements of others, to accept and admire the ways of God in other persons and other institutions.

This is precisely what happens in ecumenical hospitality. Whatever title observers from another church are given officially, they need to enter into the mind of the gathering to which they are sent in order to understand its purpose, its proceedings, its deliberate conclusions and its unspoken implications. This requires creating a space in one's mind where information will be received and processed. It is doubtful that one's mind can assimilate the thoughts and the mode of worship of another Christian group unless it is prompted to do so by a heartfelt desire for reconciliation and unity in Christ, and by a readiness to take whatever intermediary steps towards such unity may be necessary.

The observers who attended Vatican Council II at the invitation of John XXIII were aware of representing their own church with its history, its doctrinal and moral teaching, its liturgy and its theology, its structures, its accumulated memory of centuries of separation, in some cases its resentment for past persecution and its lingering distrust of others, and also its more recent ecumenical experience. The observers were welcomed, and several theologians were designated to assist them. Their presence, their shared reflections on the conciliar debates, their exchanges of views with members of the council (chiefly with members and consultants of the Pontifical Secretariat for Promoting Christian Unity), the lectures that some of them gave to various groups of bishops – all these made a positive contribution to the updating of the Catholic church that Pope John XXIII saw as the general purpose of the council. The Eastern Orthodox, Oriental Orthodox, Anglican, Protestant and Old Catholic observers fully met the hopes of their hosts as they contributed to the council with discernment and generosity.

The council was undoubtedly an extraordinary event outside the usual forms of everyday activity in the churches. It nonetheless may serve as an indicator of theological fruits that may be expected from ecumenical hospitality: not only better mutual knowledge through study and appreciation, but also mutual enrichment through giving and receiving. What observers and their interlocutors may experience at the individual level should be acknowledged by church leaders.

Through careful education and pastoral care, it also should be shared by the ordinary Christian faithful in congregations and parishes.

One way to introduce congregations and parishes to the desire for Christian unity has been to bring believers of different churches together, not only for social concerns and witness, but also on the occasions of weddings, funerals, retreats, Bible studies, preaching and teaching. Even where hospitality in regard to sacraments seems bound to remain partial, the sharing of the word of God read, preached and studied is widely possible in congregations, in seminaries and in other venues.

Remaining questions – an incentive to deeper dialogue

Ecumenical hospitality raises a number of theological questions that need to be examined in dialogue so that eventually they may be answered by churches together. The most urgent among these questions derives from the current problem of eucharistic hospitality: Should ecumenical hospitality imply eucharistic hospitality because it is Christ himself who invites to communion? Or is unity in communion with Christ inseparable from unity in the visible communion of the church? As already mentioned, this is where the churches of Orthodox/Catholic tradition differ from the churches of the Reformation as to the theological positions that need to be resolved through dialogue.

Another problem, related to the first, concerns the recognition of ministry. Strictly speaking, denying "validity" to another church's ministry does not deny that the ministry in question carries the fruits of the Spirit. It simply records the fact that some churches do not see their own standards of ordination in some other churches. From their separate traditions and varied understandings of the nature of the church, they have inherited such different criteria for ministry and diverse forms of ordination that their distinctive systems seem to be mutually incompatible. But what seems incompatible to people well may be included in the purpose of God.

A third problem needs to be faced by many churches. Why should they still do separately what they easily could do together? One could go one step further and ask, why not decide to live together in ecclesial communion, so that pending questions might be answered and problems solved by the experience of common life in the Body of Christ? Some might respond readily to this approach, while other churches would view this proposal as contrary to convictions of faith held in conscience.

Because it puts these questions in sharp focus, ecumenical hospitality should be a strong incentive to deeper theological dialogue among the churches.

5. Hospitality When It Is Practised Well

Ecumenical hospitality derives from our oneness in Christ. It speaks to a desire to welcome the other as Christ has welcomed us for the glory of God (Rom. 15:7). The adjective "ecumenical" implies a movement towards the visible unity of Christians. The motive force of such movement is love. In this movement towards unity, this acceptance of the other, how do we practise hospitality, that generous and open welcome of fellow Christians with whom we do not yet share full, visible communion? This chapter proposes to describe some things that host and guest in ecumenical relationships should be aware of, and suggest ways to increase the spirit of hospitality in our churches today. Our purpose is to describe what is possible rather than to prescribe rules to follow.

In some cases, we may be called upon to exercise the duties of host or guest because of a clear invitation; at other times, an occasion may arise unexpectedly where one finds oneself a host. While it is not possible to anticipate every situation, what follows are some principles, attitudes and examples to help the reader understand what is meant by ecumenical hospitality in its practical application.

Some general themes in ecumenical hospitality

Forethought and adaptability

The obvious first step by a host in offering hospitality is to be aware of one's guests and their needs. If Christian brothers and sisters have been invited to a liturgical ceremony, or a prayer service, or a conference where as guests they may be unfamiliar with the rubrics of a service or the behaviour expected from participants, the host has a responsibility to try to anticipate any social awkwardness that might arise. For example, what text will be used for the Lord's prayer? What is a proper response to the acclamation, "Christ has risen"? How, if appropriate, should participants share in the Lord's supper? Rubrics for ceremonies and texts should be printed and made available so that the guests can adapt and fit in to an unfamiliar situation. Likewise guests must be ready to adapt to a situation where the usual boundaries in services (e.g., between laity and clergy) are different from their own traditions. It may be advisable to have a special host to assist in particular situations. Special attention may be needed, for example, from celibate clergy as they consider appropriate ways to receive spouses of married clergy, who also may be attending the event: Where are they to be seated? What place of honour do they have?

How is one a good host or a good guest? Be aware and be ready to adapt! It is clear that, since the host has invited, the heavier responsibility of hospitality falls on the host, but the guest also has responsibilities. In speaking of hospitality, then, we recognize that the responsibilities of host and guest differ but both have to be aware of their roles and be ready to adapt to the situation. We can distinguish, obviously, between adapting to religious or social situations and compromising some principle of practice and doctrine. A guest should never be asked to do the latter, but can reasonably be expected to make some adjustments in the former.

In our discussion here, we have been talking about those situations where the status of host and guest is clear to both. In the course of the ecumenical age, who is guest and who is host may not always appear obvious. In such unstructured situations, which some might call "accidental ecumenism", the principles of awareness and adaptability hold sway; one may not be sure whether one is guest or host, yet each person is called on to be aware of the duty of welcoming the other in discussion and adapting to the situation in humility.

Ecumenical meetings, commissions and dialogues, occasions for common scriptural study, or opportunities for churches to address their common social and cultural life – these have become so familiar and take place so often that it is not always clear who is host and who is guest. An important principle to be observed here is that joint ecumenical enterprises should be planned and carried out jointly. That is, one Christian group does not plan a whole project or ceremony and then request another Christian group to tag along to "make it ecumenical". Hospitality provides the occasion to exercise Christ-like service, not to exert power.

Recognition

If we take for granted the presence of those whom we invite to our prayer or social gathering, then we are not treating them as guests, or giving them proper welcome. We do not ignore guests who come to our homes. Some sort of recognition that they are guests is required. So it is in ecumenical settings.

Ecumenical guests are not a kind of ornament we add to make our ceremony more impressive or to foster an impression of broad-mindedness. The invitees are our brothers and sisters in Christ. Thus, it is not enough, for example, to *invite* an ecumenical delegation to a liturgical service; it is important to make a *public recognition* that these guests are brothers and sisters, with whom we share many of the riches of Christ's gift to humanity. It can be helpful to stress very simply these common gifts: our baptism in Christ, our love of and obedience to his word, our common appreciation of prayer in Christ. In other words, hospitable recognition of guests is not just publicly acknowledging their presence, but also pointing out their connections with the hosts. Recognizing someone's presence is common courtesy; recognizing his or her connection in Christ is the mark of ecumenical hospitality. Such recognition "teaches" others more eloquently than any document that we are brothers and sisters in the Lord.

Planning counters awkwardness

It is not surprising that some awkwardness can arise in a casual social situation that is new to its participants. This is true even more in ecumenical encounters where sensitivity is heightened and where more is at stake, namely receiving the other as Christ. Being aware of potential awkwardness is important; a little instruction beforehand of those being welcomed by those receiving can prevent people from feeling out of place. Even simple actions like walking into a church building can be puzzling for the stranger: What sort of reverence do I show? Where do I sit? Is silence called for? Many guests in ecumenical social situations are unclear about the distinctions between and among church traditions, or are unfamiliar with clergy/lay distinctions. Some people shy away from ecumenical encounters since they fear they are not "experts" in theology. Perhaps they are embarrassed by their slim understanding of their own tradition. It falls to those inviting to be sure the social situation does not devolve into a comprehensive exam! We all need to be conscious, for example, that a term used in one tradition does not necessarily carry the same sense in another. Hosts should feel free to be "proactive" and set expectations about the process for the meeting and the degree of participation with which each group is comfortable. Let guests know that it is all right to ask questions they might fear would sound stupid. Be ready to diffuse awkwardness when things go awry.

It is helpful for hosts and guests to inform themselves as well as they can about what is expected of them and to explore, for example, customs with which they are comfortable (or the reverse) in an ecumenical prayer service. The desire for unity should be visible in such a situation. It is better not to insist on one form of prayer that others have difficulty in accepting. Planning, then, is a sign of ecumenical hospitality. It allows the parties to participate as fully as they desire, and it gives them permission to "go deeper" in their relationship in Christ.

Levels of ecumenical awareness

In extending hospitality to the other we can look at our Christian welcome from four different perspectives and live in all four levels at the same time.

Personal awareness

How do I in my personal attitudes feel about the other? If someone is unknown to me personally, or comes from a tradition with which I have only the slightest knowledge, how do I relate to that person, whether I am host or guest? This personal trajectory calls on me to take stock of my attitudes towards those who are not members of my tradition in communion of mind and heart. What assumptions do I make about the other? Why do I wish to engage in conversation (or prayer) with the other? What demands will this relationship with the other make on me? This perspective does not just end with questions; it can move to a more interpersonal awareness.

Interpersonal awareness

When men and women from different Christian traditions develop friendships through conversation and shared faith experiences, the previously unknown attitudes and beliefs of the other become known; acquaintances in dialogue become friends in the Lord. The trust, respect and openness that are part of friendship may enable them to explore more deeply the nuances of their traditions in ways that are beneficial not only to their friendship, but also to their churches. Faith commitments remain the same for both, but their faith has been enlarged and the prayer of Jesus (John 17:21) takes on fresh significance.

Institutional awareness

When those who in some way represent their churches or traditions are in a position to establish a public set of practices and customs for ecumenical hospitality, they have power to inform and shape the attitudes, beliefs and behaviours of individuals and institutions in ways that potentially enhance the quest for Christian unity. In these situations, people are not speaking for themselves alone, but also for the tradition, office and polity from which they come.

This perspective enlarges the personal one; it does not contradict it, at least in theory. People are chosen to represent their tradition because they accept it, are convinced of it and wish to proclaim it. But the context of this representation is public, not private. They are aware that not all within their church may share an attitude of concern for or welcome of the other. The "professional" frequently speaks in a context of public indifference born of ignorance rather than in a situation of fervent longing for Christian unity. Conscious that one is speaking not merely for oneself, the professional has the opportunity to model a clearer, more conscious sense of welcome.

Cultural awareness

Many churches have customary ways of dealing with other churches that are rooted in tradition and cultural practice. These established patterns provide guidance in a variety of situations, but sometimes the patterns need to be re-examined to see if they are, indeed, the best possible ways to offer ecumenical hospitality. Such self-examination may be called for especially in situations when one church may be in a numerical majority and the other(s) are in a minority. It is not the numerical size of a denomination, nor the social standing of its members, nor the political power or cultural prestige it enjoys that should draw Christians to each other, but the understanding of and living out our faith in Christ and our call to reconciliation. Social conditions may call for further awareness on the part of the hosts and some education in matters ecumenical to help churches move beyond tolerance and social politeness to real ecumenical hospitality.

* * *

These four spheres of awareness are not moments in a linear process. One does not move from personal, to interpersonal, to institutional and cultural awareness as along a straight road. Rather, these are various aspects of awareness that individuals may develop in particular situations. If any linear movement may be discerned, it is one that goes from friendship to trust to institutional acceptance.

Some qualities of ecumenical hospitality

Although it is not possible to identify every possible situation where ecumenical hospitality is called for, it is possible to name certain qualities that should characterize a welcoming ecumenical spirit, whatever the situation.

Strive for honesty and transparency

When striving to understand the other, one should be respectful and direct. Whether people represent themselves or their churches, sharing insights about their church's tradition, teaching or practice is basic. Sly insinuations about another's beliefs or practices undermine the possibility for healthy dialogue. The partners in interpersonal ecumenical relations respond best when no suspicions or innuendos cloud the atmosphere. Let a "yes" be a "yes" and a "no" be a "no".

Assume the best, not the worst

It is very easy in dialogue (as well as in other situations) to compare "my" best with "your" worst. It is natural to compare one's own ideal with another's practice and find the latter wanting. This is a temptation to be resisted whether one is host or guest. Comparisons based on insufficient evidence or incomplete understanding turn a welcome into a judgment, often resulting in anger rather than love. In discussion it is helpful to try to understand exactly what the other is saying or doing. If it does not seem consistent with one's own view, seek additional information in an effort to comprehend the other's perspective. If this is not possible, then let the experience stand as a point of disagreement to be explored further at an appropriate time.

Understand one's own tradition

Knowing one's tradition provides a level of comfort in meeting the other. Christians do not have to be specialists in religious practice or doctrine in order to share their beliefs, practices of prayer or convictions. It is important, however, to have a good grasp of the fundamentals of one's faith and an ability to explain the basics. The purpose of such knowledge is not to proselytize but to enlighten, not to make hurtful comparisons but to help another to understand. In fact, one of the potentially exhilarating fruits of ecumenical encounter is that it encourages participants to delve more deeply into their own tradition.

Practise humility

As trust develops between Christians of different traditions, they find it more comfortable – even safer – to reveal their own concerns and to become more transparent. It is easier to place oneself in the shoes of another, to be sympathetic, when another's church suffers humiliation or disaster.

Humility allows individuals to continue to interact even when churches are divided over hotly contentious issues, such as abortion, the ordination of women, the propriety of gay marriage or the ordination of practising homosexuals. Humility says that we may expect some awkwardness in welcoming the stranger; it is not that our welcome is provisional but incomplete. We recognize our differences, and they do impose limits (e.g. reception of communion), but even then we can acknowledge the pain of our separation and pray for healing in the body of Christ.

Humility allows us to work towards the healing of memories from past conflicts between churches. Although the source of the original conflict may have disappeared, grudges and rancour often remain: "you" are one of "them". An honest assessment of church history suggests that all churches have fallen short of Christian charity at one time or another, and have shameful episodes along with moments of honour.

Understanding this helps us transcend past failures and present shortcomings, and enables us to welcome the other in a spirit of humility before our common Lord and Saviour.

When in the gospel accounts a person encounters Christ, a change occurs in those who welcome his words, whether they are words of invitation or warning, teaching or compassion. Rarely do those who welcome Christ remain the same. They are changed by their encounter with the Lord. Even their sense of the divine may be expanded.

Can we allow for the possibility of change in the encounter between a guest and host? No particular transformation is expected; welcoming one another, however, does not leave host or guest untouched. Ecumenical hospitality brings with it the risk and promise of change. Humility prompts us to run that risk of beginning a new relationship, to find new possibilities in each new encounter.

A postscript

Because of progress made through the ecumenical movement, it is not uncommon now for Christian clergy and laity to be invited to attend a religious service held in a house of worship other than their own. The occasion may be a service of morning or evening prayer, a baptism, marriage or funeral, or a service of installation or ordination. In some contexts, the eucharist may be celebrated.

The invitation to participate in the worship of another tradition may offer the opportunity to include a guest in the ceremony. Each tradition has its own norms about these occasions, and both host and guest should be informed about these norms and follow them. Thus at a baptism, for example, one tradition may allow a

Christian from another tradition to serve as godparent, while another tradition may not. This latter situation, while difficult for those involved, should not be construed as a slight or a judgment on the guest's worthiness. Rather, it is a painful recognition of the current understanding among various churches about what visible unity means and how it can be achieved.

Perhaps nowhere does this difference of meaning and concomitant distress stand out more plainly than in the issue of eucharistic sharing. Here we must acknowledge the pain of the churches' divisions so evident at the Lord's table. We cannot be satisfied with simple acquiescence to the de facto condition of the church of Christ. We must acknowledge the fact that our worship falls short of Christ's deepest desire that all may be one. While we are called to respect one another's traditions and sacramental understandings, Christians may seize these occasions to recognize the limits of our unity thus far, and as a spur to pray and work for the full visible unity of all who follow Christ. Attention to every possible expression of ecumenical hospitality by the host in these settings is especially appreciated by guests, and significantly can channel any pain experienced into positive initiatives towards Christian unity.

6. A Homiletic Reflection on Hospitality and Conversion

Giving credit where credit is due

Some would say that the present up-hill quest for Christian unity is in itself something of a miracle. This is because far too many groups of Christians from various spiritual traditions, East, West, North and South, have avoided recognizing one another as separated but real brothers and sisters. Rather than seek healing, reconciliation and unity, separation was justified because the faith, actions and perhaps the very person of the "other" was viewed as significantly inferior for various reasons.

That Christianity today is visibly fragmented into various divisions, sub-divisions and groups, large and small, should not surprise us. Group psychology studies generally attest to the fact that the cohesion of groups tends to disintegrate over the course of time, after their fundamental uniting vision is divided even once! A process of disintegration and fragmentation begins that eventually breeds more and more splintering until the group is no longer viable. Through the course of church history, numerous breaks or schisms have occurred that, when left unattended, have led to other divisions.

Until rather recently, Christianity had experienced so many of these divisions that it is a wonder that Christians are still recognizable as a viable body in the world at all. Sadly, during this present season some have called an "ecumenical winter", many of these divisions remain even as new ones appear to be in the making. Nevertheless, the rise and prolonged effort of the ecumenical movement has caused many Christians to take pause and reconsider these divisions. Personal and ecclesial bridges have begun to be built; relationships have been restored; and in some places even significant healing has already begun. Perhaps we can say that, from the perspective of group psychology, this phenomenon of growing (albeit uneven) Christian unity should not be happening!

The hospitality of God:
a revolutionary understanding

To what may we give credit for this apparent impossibility? While the present success of the ecumenical movement rests upon the effort of countless persons, the final reason for this burgeoning fruitfulness lies well outside of us. For this, we are obliged to give glory and thanks to the "good and benevolent God who loves humankind".[17] This ecumenical effort is the human response to the God who loved us first, and who still keeps reaching out to us first. This loving God has empowered and under-girded the quest for Christian unity.

Nothing in creation even compares to the hospitality of God! The triune God's invitation to us is not formal or perfunctory; it is not tentative or timid; nor is it unenthusiastic or conditional. Scandalous as it may sound, the living God of love invites each of us to enjoy complete fellowship with him as adopted sons and daughters. In many ways, God's seeking to share God's "home" with us is not unlike the behaviour of a beggar desperately seeking our love. God begs us to join him by loving him and thus one another.

During the late 6th to early 7th century St Maximos the Confessor bore witness to this astounding teaching: "God made himself a beggar by reason of his concern for us... suffering mystically through his tenderness to the end of time according to the measure of each one's suffering."[18]

The ineffable God, while mysteriously fully present within creation and abiding eternally outside of time and space, is in countless ways a "fool" in love with us!

This teaching helps us put into perspective the ancient Christian affirmation that "the Word became a human person, so that the human person may become divine". God was so "foolish" as to utterly empty himself *(ekenosen eauton)* (Phil. 2:7) and become one of us, one with us, God Emmanuel. There are no conditions to this love. Creation will never be the same again. The living God of love freely initiated this inexpressibly unique and astounding action, in order to restore our broken relationship with him and all creation due to human sin and fallenness.

With this in mind, it is not merely for religious or ethical obligation that our Lord offers us the greatest commandment: "You shall love the Lord your God with all your heart, with all your soul and with all of your mind and with all your strength... You shall love your neighbour as yourself" (Mark 12:30-31). Jesus' reason for giving us this prime directive is far more personal or, more accurately, interpersonal! In order for us as individual persons and as members of the church to take up our abode in eternal communion with this divine "fool", we too, are called to imitate God in Christ.

Reflecting upon this in light of the historical progress of the ecumenical endeavour, we can appreciate how the quest for unity, likewise, tends to make "fools" of us. Any action, particularly conscious gestures of hospitality towards persons who were previously considered "strangers", challenges the institutionalized status quo of hard-hearted, conventional separation. These gestures are typically treated as "foolish", at least at first.

We must call to mind here the countless faithful and courageous Christians who, while situated in their respective traditions and particular life contexts, took issue with the apparent status quo and facilitated the progress of church unity. Some were well-known church leaders, ecumenical officers, pastors, theologians, educators, activists, writers, administrators and professional staff people. Most were thoughtful and faithful believers, perhaps not unlike some of our own grandparents, who sacrificed to love their neighbours as themselves, despite enormous challenges and consequences. To these people we express our special gratitude and our profound debt. This is because as few as three or four generations ago, most would not have even recognized each other as separated yet fellow believers.

"Many are called, yet few are chosen" (Matt. 20:16).

Can we ask ourselves the question: What is it that keeps us divided *today*? Even though this question poses another, perhaps unending topic of investigation, we would benefit greatly by honestly asking ourselves this question from time to time. By thoughtfully so doing, we may once again come face to face with some aspect of our own inner unfinished business, brokenness or hardness of heart. This added discipline may offer us new insights into how we may improve our efforts of reaching out to other Christians, particularly through our gestures of hospitality.

Because of this self-evaluative process, we can learn more about what may impede or assist our effort for renewed and more authentic relationships. In assisting us with this self-examination, we would do well to remember the ancient adage made famous by Saint Maximos the Confessor: "Nothing has caused divisions in the church more than the fact that we do not love one another."[19] It is the very same, astounding human failing of lack of love that has kept us from one another *and* from falling into the arms of the divine Fool who longingly waits for us to commune with him.

Truly, many Christians think they desire to love God and others. Perhaps they do. Cultivating this desire, however, is much, much harder than it seems, as "it is a fearful thing to fall into the hands of the living God" (Heb. 10:31). By striving to befriend God, we risk the end of life as we know it. There are no certainties on this path. This is because, as we seek out the beloved divine Fool who fashioned us, we realize once again that we are not the ones who define who we are. Instead, we wait continuously, with extreme sacrificial patience, alert, hands open and outstretched, offering our personal identities as cherished sons and daughters as defined by the sacrificial love of the Most High God, ready to receive the unending gift from the divine Other.

In some ways, our seeking God is not unlike our being little hatchlings waiting eagerly in the nest, mouths open, tiny wings fluttering, stretching out to receive nourishment. They wait with desperation for their mother, who offers them their sustenance. The mother-bird's unconditional "hospitality" is a matter of life and death for her hatchlings. Such is the offering of God's "sustenance" towards us. This is a God whose hospitality offers us God's very self. For all humankind, this is likewise a matter of abundant life or spiritual death (cf. Matt. 10:39).

This life-long effort of consciously seeking the living God of love is a universe away from today's assumption, popular among many, that asserts, "This is what I am, take it or leave it!" This strident declaration depicts a virtual independence from the love of the living God and encapsulates the essence of the fatal sin of pride that is the desire to be god without God.

By pursuing instead the "narrow path", we willingly risk our selves, as we surrender consciously the very

core of our identity into the hands of the One who created us. Clearly, we are not in charge of this journey!
For many of us, this effort may sometimes feel like an
indescribable, terminal loving sacrifice, at other times
like a crucifixion.

Nevertheless, the reward is infinitely greater than the
relatively small personal price paid. This is where we
engage the journey harnessed by the "sweet yoke" (Matt.
11:30). It is in pursuing the path that leads to joyful "life
in abundance" (John 10:10), as we discover the personal
vocation to which each of us has been called. This call is
reflected in the ancient direction of St Gregory of Sinai,
who seven centuries ago instructed Christians:

> Become what you already are,
> Find him who is already yours,
> Listen to him who never ceases speaking to you,
> Possess him who already possesses you.[20]

What does this have to say about unity to Christians from various traditions?

More changes and upheavals have occurred in the
past ten to fifteen years than could have been imagined
before. We faithfully must bear in mind that despite
human sin, the living Triune God rises to every occasion, in God's way and time. God is not bound by
human timetables, demands and objectives. Nothing,
not a single thing, escapes the attention of the God of
love. It is we human beings who miserably fail God and
one another.

In order to continue on the path towards church
unity, our personal participation in this movement
must be assessed frequently. New challenges, new
options, new relationships, new commitments, new
responsibilities, new resources, new objectives will
present themselves, as we make our choices and as

time unfolds about us. This process is hazardous in and of itself, but this may reflect only the easier part of this adventure.

The difficulties arrive when we come face to face with the depths of our own fears, attachments and hardheartedness. We are afraid to acknowledge certain parts of ourselves, even to our own selves, as these impede our growth towards God and one another. We are afraid of losing forever that which is familiar to us. Furthermore, we would then have to be open to welcome the "foreigner" and the "stranger". Are our hearts able to contain all that?

Nevertheless, what God requires of us is precisely to summon up the courage to surrender impediments that compromise our progress. We can be sure that, as we strive to direct our lives in this manner, life sometimes may present us with unexpected opportunities inviting us to discernment. These opportunities no doubt will include taking uncomfortable risks. Some of these may be small and some great. They may include personal change, vulnerability, exposure or loss. These risks may involve appearing foolish to friends, family and the powers-that-be. Sometimes these risks will have enduring consequences. The witness of St Paul encourages us regarding the ways of God for our lives. He reminds us, "God's foolishness is wiser than human wisdom, and God's weakness is stronger than human strength" (1 Cor. 1:25).

Pursuing this direction will bring us to decisions and courses of action that sometimes defy conventional wisdom, causing us to appear foolish. Such is the case for the ways of God. "Where is the one who is wise? Where is the scribe? Where is the debater of this age? Has not God made foolish the wisdom of the world?" (1 Cor. 1:20). Christian unity is possible only for such "fools". The Great Fool, our divine Beloved, even now begs us to imitate and follow him.

If the deep desire for Christian unity is to increase its hold on our churches and traditions, it first must occur personally within each of our hearts. Each of us, from our respective spiritual traditions, is invited to prepare our own hearts and lives knowing that we may be taking on foolishness itself. New commitments may be discerned that cause us to reach out and receive the other in new-found gestures of welcome and hospitality. By so doing, we prepare to receive the Great Fool, who is also the Author of Life, and hence the Architect of Unity. For the miracle of unity to occur, our previous personal conventions no longer will be adequate.

A vocation of foolishness, a merciful heart

With divine assistance, each of us can summon the courage to foster this eternally new walk with Christ. Perhaps a unique characteristic of this quest, quite absurd to the conventional world, will be that this journey will cultivate within us a merciful heart. A truly merciful heart makes no sense. Perhaps it even defies the *status quo*, since it expresses love from within the very heart of God. To our indescribable surprise, however, the human heart miraculously may contain the love of God, of others, even of creation itself.

Writing in the 4th century, St Gregory of Nyssa reminded Christians of this amazing assertion. Through the wisdom and folly of God, our very hearts are able to contain him. Our very beings are created to be hospitable to God. We need only "look at him". St Gregory wrote,

Realize how much your Creator has honoured you above all creatures. He did not make the heavens in his image, nor the moon, the sun, the beauty of the stars or anything else which surpasses understanding. You alone are a reflection of eternal beauty, a receptacle of happiness, an image of the true light. And, if you look at him, you will become what he is, imitating him who shines within you, whose glory is reflected in your purity. Nothing in the entire creation can equal your grandeur. All the heavens can fit into the palm of the hand of God... Although he is so great that he can hold all creation in his palm, you can wholly embrace him. He dwells within you.[21]

Even with our very best efforts, this amazing gift will not take place as a result of our own doing, but rather through the divinely desperate interventions of the Beloved Fool. Writing also about the merciful heart, St Isaac the Syrian of Nineveh taught in the 7th century,

And what is a merciful heart: The burning of the heart on account of all creation, on account of people and birds and animals and demons, and for every created being. Because of their remembrance, the eyes fill with tears. Great and intense mercy grasps the heart and wrings it out, for the person who is merciful is not able to bear or hear or see any harm, or the slightest sorrow taking place in the created world. This holds true on behalf of those who harm him. For these, the person offers prayers continually with tears for their protection and redemption. He does so even for the snakes that crawl upon the ground. All of this the person does out of his great mercy, which moves in his heart without measure in the likeness of God.[22]

Today Christian unity is needed desperately in order to proclaim the love of God for the whole world. In the end, the unity of the church will not serve us, those who consciously know ourselves to be beloved members of one another. Rather, it will foster the love of others and of all creation.

Through the gracious activity of the Holy Spirit, we are called in our personal journey to seek Christ first in every relationship and through every aspect of life. By pursuing this path, we may find that it not only leads us to Christ, but also to one another. We pray that all will experience the hospitality of God and find their true home in him.

7. The Fruits of Ecumenical Hospitality

A priest had a small vegetable garden next to his church. Each year he dutifully enriched the soil and waited. It took several years, but eventually everything began to flourish in that garden. The garden had gone from being a mediocre sandy plot to being an extremely hospitable bed for seeds of any type.

In similar fashion, ecumenical hospitality can create a good seedbed where works that promote the unity of the Christian church can flourish and make possible joint service to the world. As people offer or receive the gift of hospitality, they open themselves to the possibility of being transformed through the Holy Spirit. Transformation enables us to see other Christians and their churches in a fresh light. It may enhance our longing for unity. The quality of trust that develops in such interpersonal encounters provides the possibility for change in our churches.

Yes, patience is necessary, just as it is when we nourish the soil in a garden. However, in this process Christians together begin to see themselves in a larger context – both in the church and in the world. Ecumenical hospitality creates a seedbed for correcting imbalance and distortion in our perceptions of other Christians' teaching, polity, worship and social witness. We are reminded that we may not have the whole picture; that we have gifts to share with each other. And these promising signs in the quest for Christian unity offer hope to the human community, which in so many ways suffers division and conflict.

When such a seedbed for ecumenical relationships is not present, the possibilities for mutual enrichment from differing spiritual traditions are limited. Theological and scriptural scholarship is constricted. Above all, the churches are hindered in any joint action as they attempt to respond to a community or world in crisis.

During the course of this project, members of the drafting group found themselves telling stories and listening more intently to the stories of others. What follows is a sampling of these stories. We have chosen these few examples from our own experiences and encounters. They demonstrate the great impact that a history of ecumenical hospitality can have as churches act together on behalf of the world. We hope that these few illustrations will inspire the reader to reflect on his or her own experiences, and to build on these examples of ecumenical hospitality.

Transformation through interpersonal relationships

Both the Hebrew and Christian scriptures teach us that the most important thing on which human beings should focus is relationships with those around us. It is in the midst of these relationships that we find ourselves, others and God. Often we meet the other across a divide separated by faith, expressions of faith or of faith experiences to which we do not subscribe or with which we are not comfortable. If we are open, however, such meetings can provoke new dimensions of the experience of Christ and God. They can draw us towards what really constitutes the heart of a truth previously seen only through the lens of our own Christian tradition.

A Roman Catholic member of our drafting group offered testimony to the transforming power of interpersonal relationships among Christians. He said, "Since ordination, I have worked with Protestant laity and clergy on numerous community issues in six different suburban or urban areas, in which we have seen each other's personal strengths and weaknesses. I have been part of weekly scripture study with Protestant clergy for almost forty years. This has helped me to expand my appreciation of our common understanding of the scriptures. A few years ago, I had an extended exposure to Russian Orthodox prayer at a retreat in London, England. That experience opened me to the mystical, non-cerebral dimension of prayer. Initially I rejected this, but after sticking with the experience of Orthodox prayer, I eventually was able to surrender to it. This opened up new possibilities of prayer I had previously not explored."

Another member of our group recounted a story she had heard recently. A priest found himself hospitalized with a potentially life-threatening illness. Few people were aware of his plight, but it happened that a Unitarian minister – a member of an ecumenical clergy group – was making pastoral calls in the hospital shortly after the priest's admittance. He told the story weeks later, when the prognosis had improved and he was back on his feet. The hospitalized priest had been dozing, and when he opened his eyes, there was Joe, standing over his bed, embodying compassion. They talked. Joe prayed for his brother. And thus began a deepening friendship which prompted far-ranging conversations dispelling stereotypes and deepening appreciation of the traditions represented by these two clergy.

A Romanian Orthodox colleague from Geneva reported that, since 1975 when a congregation named fot the feast day of "The Resurrection of the Lord" was established in Chambésy near Geneva, each Sunday divine liturgy has been celebrated. The Romanian language normally is used; but if the priest notices that non-Romanian Orthodox or visitors from other Christian traditions are in the congregation, he makes an effort to adapt the language so that the liturgy is accessible to all who are present. At the conclusion of the service, he specifically welcomes the guests – in his words, "a small act of ecumenical hospitality" that can have a powerful experience of welcome for the worshippers.

Another working group member said, "In towns in our diocese where I have been assigned, I have observed and seen the wisdom of other forms of church. My experience of their governance structure has moved me to help create more collaborative structures in the parishes where I have worked. Because of this exposure and involvement, I now experience myself as a more balanced Christian than I was years ago. I am more aware of my previous unconscious, reactive stances and practices that hindered ecumenical relationships for myself and for the people with whom I worked. I am freer to partner with Christians from other churches on community issues. I experience myself as more authentic in leadership in my own community. I am better able to represent the entire church as I offer leadership in the civic community. I am aware that if I am to be an authentic Christian leader, I must carry within my prayer, word and action a sensitivity to the gifts that are carried – and sometimes better developed – by other Christian communions, as well as the gifts and emphases of my own communion."

A colleague recounted the experience of visiting a monastery of Orthodox women in Romania. When he was about to leave, the sisters "accompanied me to the train station. They waited with me until the train came, got onto the train with me to make sure that I got to my seat all right, and explained to the people in my cabin that I was from Canada, spoke English and French but not Romanian, and asked them to assist me should I need help with anything. Then one of the sisters opened her bag and lifted out a package of food copious enough to last for three days! And another sister, who had returned to the car, suddenly reappeared with a bouquet of fresh flowers from their garden." He concluded, "I thought I knew what graciousness and hospitality were, but I had been surprised by grace."

Correcting personal imbalances and developing sensitivity to the gifts of other churches do not come out of thin air. These movements in the human heart need soil, a seedbed, in which this sensitivity can find a place to grow. This soil gets worked upon jointly, shared by ecumenical partners, some of whom may become friends. In this process, people show each other true ecumenical hospitality.

Ecumenical hospitality leading to breakthroughs in relationships among churches

In 1999 the Lutheran World Federation and the Roman Catholic Church signed the Joint Declaration on the Doctrine of Justification. They came to an agreement that anathemas these churches had hurled at each other over several centuries concerning the doctrine of salvation need no longer apply. These two churches agreed that while salvation comes through faith, an authentic faith life shows itself in good works. While there was recognition that this agreement certainly did not resolve all the differences between the two churches, both recognized that on this fundamental issue, which had been a major cause for the great split in the church in the 16th century, these churches had taken a monumental step along the road towards Christian unity.

How did this happen? As with so many other ecumenical breakthroughs, it occurred through years of official dialogues by representatives of the two churches, in which they met in each other's spaces in reciprocal acts of hospitality. They not only talked together, but they also shared meals together. They worshipped together. They took walks in "off hours", talking about all sorts of things. They drank together. They told stories. They debated. They argued. They laughed. And gradually, they came to appreciate and trust each other in ways that enabled them to work through what previously had seemed like intractable differences.

As with all official agreements between churches – whether steps along the way to reconciliation, or actions enabling "full communion" among churches – the agreements begin to raise questions in all church settings about how Christians should relate to and see each other in the light of new agreements. It should raise questions in places where social service offices co-exist: are there ways churches could stop duplicating services and collaborate to serve the poor better? Such steps would give visible witness to churches living out a response to Christ's call to his followers to be one.

Official changes that come from ecumenical hospitality can produce the fruit of movement towards Christian unity at many levels of the church. One church may see more clearly the need for lay participation in policy decisions at all levels. Another church may find a word from God on the proper balance between public and private prayer. A third church may hear a word that will diminish its irritation or refusal to respect another church because of its style of prayer (formula or free prayer) or its approach to scriptural interpretation.

In regions with increasingly diverse populations of Christian believers, some churches have responded to the exhortation to "receive one another" by literally opening their doors. At a Presbyterian church (PCUSA) in Cambridge, Massachusetts, USA, the church building is shared by four groups of worshippers – the Presbyterian congregation, a congregation from Haiti, a

Chinese fellowship and a gathering of Presbyterians from Brazil. A Presbyterian elder reports that "going beyond building use and cultural idiosyncrasies is a first step. Moving into a place of mutual respect and ecumenical friendship is a goal that has required time, prayer, and the commitment of church leaders. We still are in process, but we are making progress."

Ecumenical hospitality may help us to let go of a definition of the final unity of the church in its full visible form. It prepares us to wait in hope with other Christians for the gift from God of full or complete unity that is our baptismal promise and call. When we practise such hospitality we prepare a proper seedbed that will be receptive to that gift of unity whenever and however it comes to us from God.

Examples of the relationship between ecumenical hospitality and social justice

A story of African American churches

Sometimes ecumenical hospitality provides refuge for the oppressed and initiative for change that extends far beyond the initial participants. The civil rights movement of the 1950s and 1960s in the United States, led most notably by Dr Martin Luther King, Jr, was first of all a movement originating in the black churches. It was facilitated by the ecumenical hospitality practised by black Christians to one another. This three hundred year old movement within black churches from different traditions in the United States created a common awareness of the injustices with which black people lived.

Moses leading his people out of slavery, God freeing Daniel from the lions' den, and the vision of the dry bones in Ezekiel – all these were scripture texts used by black clergy in their congregations to sustain hope for freedom from injustice and oppression.

The strong, clear biblical images in the addresses of Dr Martin Luther King, Jr, and the response of black people in all settings to the civil rights movement, emanated from within the ecumenical movement. These initiatives eventually prompted other churches and the United States government to respond positively to this cry for justice, ending legal segregation in all its forms, promoting fairness in the workplace, the voting booth and other settings.

A story of churches in Korea

From the beginning of the Korean Protestant missionary movement the Christian churches in Korea have followed the patterns of denominationalism that echo Western Europe and North America. Yet from 1905 the Presbyterians and Methodists, who constitute the majority of Korean churches, have cooperated for Bible translation, hymnody, medical service, education and YMCA – YWCA activities. This spirit of cooperation has set the basic orientation for ecumenicity in Korea. The subsequent ecumenical movement, spearheaded by the Korean National Council of Churches in the mid-20th century and allied with the World Council of Churches, has represented the spirit of prophetic social concern under the phrase *missio Dei*. Together, the churches actively have been working for democratization, human rights, peaceful unification of the divided country, anti-poverty efforts and urban industrial mission.

A story of congregations in the suburban United States

In a wealthy town on the eastern seaboard of the United States, all the Christian congregations belonged to the local council of churches. In the late 1960s, following Vatican II, the clergy association began to hold "living-room dialogues" which built on a previously active Anglican-Roman Catholic conversation. The theological discussions included laity and clergy from a wide variety of congregations – Methodists, Unitarian Universalists, members of the United Church of Christ, Episcopalians, Nazarenes, Baptists and Roman Catholics. These discussions were held over seven or eight years in the homes of parishioners or in church parlours.

The Roman Catholic parish had a Christian service committee that served the poor and marginalized in the area. Despite the fact that the region was affluent, many low-income families and elderly lived in sub-standard housing. With increasing frequency these individuals and families, despite life-time residency, were forced to re-locate because of escalating housing costs.

With these years of living-room dialogues as a foundation, someone made the suggestion that the council of churches be approached about starting a Christian service committee. If they were open to the suggestion, the presenter proposed, then the Roman Catholic parish's committee would disband. The answer was quick in coming. Henceforth all the Christian churches in that town supported and served the poor by works of charity and justice through the local council of churches' Christian service committee.

Within five years, the council of churches expanded its horizons and decided to address the controversial issue of providing more low and moderate-income housing. Currently, that town has several developments for moderate and low-income elderly people and families, mentally handicapped people, with more on the way. The impetus for all of this originated among local congregations that, in the late 1960s and early 1970s, had developed strong ecumenical relationships through living room dialogues.

Ecumenical and interfaith hospitality enabled by visionary Christian leaders

In Asia

In May 1959, the world's first regional ecumenical organization, the East Asia Christian Conference (EACC) – now the Christian Conference of Asia (CCA) – came into being at a historic gathering of church leaders in Kuala Lumpur, Malaysia. Among them, somewhat to their own surprise, were official representatives of the churches of Australia and New Zealand.

Why the surprise? It was not just that geography had placed their nations well south of the Asian mainland. History, culture, politics and racism had combined to make them the region's outsiders. Fifty years ago, Asia's people were gladly divesting themselves of European colonialism and planning a new future while Australia and New Zealand still looked, thought and behaved like outposts of imperial Europe. These two countries were predominantly white and seemed determined to stay that way. Indeed, the notorious "white Australian policy", excluding Asian migrants as well as others deemed ethnically undesirable, was officially still in place. It would have been perfectly understandable and very human if Asia's churches had drawn the line south of Indonesia and left those irritatingly different white southern neighbours to go their own separate way. But they did not do so. Christian ecumenical hospitality prevailed.

Filipino Bishop Enrique Sobrepena had made it clear, at the organization's planning stage, that "we have no desire to be regarded as a colour bloc and still less as anti-European in any sense. We welcome the churches of Australia and New Zealand into the EACC because they live within the Asia area and because they symbolize, in our midst, the European churches through which we have learned our faith."

That generosity of spirit drew an enthusiastic response from the churches of Australia and New Zealand. Links with their Asian counterparts became important. Friendships deepened. Relationships proliferated. In the decades following, through the EACC (CCA), Christians of Australia and New Zealand learned a lot about the complexities of the region, the sensitivities of its people, the delicate art of ecumenical partnership. In Asian eyes, they evolved into natural, unremarkable parts of the region's Christian landscape. At home, Christians became strong advocates of better ties with these neighbours and more energetic opponents of racism in all its forms.

The bonds have held, even through times of tension. When East Timor erupted in 1999, the governments of Australia and Indonesia were growling at each other. Press and politicians on both sides were making inflammatory statements. The two armies faced the real possibility of conflict. But relations between church leaders remained strong. They were friends, and had been for years. They understood each other, and that understanding translated into trust.

In all this, the churches were far ahead of public opinion and government policy. In the mid 1990s, for example, Australia was attempting, unsuccessfully, to become a member of one of the region's intergovernmental organizations. Australian Foreign Minister Gareth Evans explained that his country, hitherto "the odd man out" in Asia, aspired to become "the odd man in". Anyone familiar with the churches' story could have been pardoned a wry smile. As far as Asia's ecumenical community was concerned, the churches of Australia and New Zealand long had been simply, unremarkably, inextricably "in" – and no odder than any of the others!

But the key was that gracious invitation, decades before.

In North America

In the fall of 1983, the then-Cardinal Joseph Bernadin, Roman Catholic Archbishop of Chicago, Illinois, convened what was to be called the Council of Religious Leaders (CRL) – an interfaith entity composed of the bishops and the executives of the mainline Christian denominations and the Jewish Federation of Synagogues. The goal of CRL was to focus on issues that the members could mutually support theologically and politically. Housing, health, education and racial reconciliation were high on the list.

In late 1984, Harold Washington was elected mayor of Chicago. This election highlighted racial divisions in the city. Some of the traditional ethnic wards banded together through their aldermen to block every legislative proposal the mayor offered. The president of the city council led the attack and vitriolic language from both sides of the city council escalated in the media. The scene grew increasingly nasty.

The crisis became the centre of attention for the members of the CRL. Discussion among the religious leaders focused on what the members could do to intervene and lower the temperature of the debate. Through its membership, the Council of Religious Leaders had easy access to both sides of the conflict.

The CRL proposed that the president of the city council, the most vociferous opponent of the mayor, meet with the mayor in a neutral setting, where they could talk face to face in a safe environment away from the attention of the public and the media. At this meeting members of the CRL sat around a long oval table. The mayor was on one side, the city council president was on the other. Cardinal Bernardin opened the meeting with a prayer. He shared with the mayor and the council president the desire of the religious leaders for civil restraint and mutual respect. The rest of the meeting was a heated dialogue between the two men in the presence of the CRL. The attacks from both sides reportedly were very personal – almost like two brothers who had been seated in the presence of their parents to vent their rage.

The political outcome was not significant. What did happen, however, was that the temperature cooled, the rhetoric changed dramatically and the atmosphere returned to more normal political bickering. The reminder that both men had religious and moral roots, symbolized by the presence of religious leaders, had called them to a slightly higher plain. The religious leaders had experienced an ability and power to speak with a united voice in the public arena. All this began because one religious leader took the initiative to be hospitable to his colleagues, and invited them to explore the unity they shared as people of faiths. In this case, the hospitality was interfaith, rather than ecumenical, but it grew out of Cardinal Bernardin's Christian sensitivity to the commitments we share through our common humanity.

Conclusion

It is the sense of our working group that God is making it increasingly clear to Christ's church that the focus of the church must be the world. Our world is increasingly divided, with growing gaps between rich and poor. It is divided by physical, economic and social violence as well as structures that enable these types of

violence to continue. This divided and violent world constantly poses questions:
- if the church is the great sacrament of the unity of Spirit, Son and Father
- if the church is the sign of the presence of God's love
- if we are commissioned by Christ to draw all to loving unity through him
- if we are to love one another and reach such unity in all our diversity, so that the world may believe in the reign of God with its values of truth, justice, love and peace.

If we believe all the foregoing statements, then is a divided church really able to fulfill the commission of Christ and follow its vocation as sign and sacrament drawing all to unity? If God has called us to be one so that the world can be one, are our divisions reinforcing resignation to the divisions in which the human family seems to be trapped?

A divided church cannot be an effective sign and servant to a divided world. Attention to matters of ecumenical hospitality smoothes the way for Christians to work together in serving the world that God loves and for which Christ died.

These few examples indicate, in diverse ways, how ecumenical hospitality can become a grace not just to the churches, but also to the world that God so loves and to which he sent his Son. These stories indicate that once ecumenical hospitality is offered and accepted, God is free to do great things in us, the churches, and through us, in the world. The fruits of this hospitality are many and at the deepest level they are God's actions, God's grace.

8. Prayers and Practical Suggestions

As members of the working group have prepared this book, we have asked ourselves what we would say or pray on various occasions when extending hospitality to ecumenical guests. The following are a few prayers and practical examples. Some we have prepared, others we have culled from the World Council of Churches. We hope these suggestions will help stimulate thinking about appropriate contexts where expressions of hospitality should be offered, and about what could be said.

Ecumenical hospitality among congregations and parishes at sacramental occasions

After all have assembled together, the leader may voice these or similar words of welcome:

Blessed is our God always, now and ever and to the ages of ages. *Amen.*

We come together from different traditions, united in the one body of Christ,
to celebrate the baptism of _____
to celebrate the marriage of_____
to honour the memory of _____

As we gather, let us recall the words of the apostle Paul:

"Let love be genuine;
    hate what is evil, hold fast to what is good;...
Rejoice in hope, be patient in tribulation, be constant in prayer... practise hospitality." (Rom. 12:9,12,13b RSV).
Whether we are hosts or guests, we are one in the Lord Jesus Christ.

Let us greet the people around us and welcome each other to this place of worship.

Prayer of confession

A prayer may be offered at the celebration of the Lord's supper/holy communion/eucharist when church canons or law do not allow eucharistic hospitality to some who are present.

O God, Holy Trinity, whose diversity reflects the nature of your unity,
we give thanks that we can come together in your presence in our diversity, sharing in this unity through our baptism.

And yet our unity is incomplete. This is painfully obvious on this day when some are able to receive the bread of life, while others are deprived of this spiritual food because of the remaining divisions among our churches.

As we celebrate this sacrament of unity, may our inability to offer hospitality at your holy table impel us all to respond with renewed vigour to the prayer of our Lord "that they may all be one... so that the world may believe...

We pray this in the name of the One who calls us to be one, our Lord Jesus Christ. *Amen.*

When one congregation offers hospitality to another in a time of adversity

Blessed is our God always, now and ever and to the ages of ages. *Amen.*

It is fitting that we come together as a Christian family at this difficult time for our brothers and sisters in Christ. We welcome you, our ecumenical guests. It is a privilege to offer you hospitality. The apostle Paul reminds us, "If one member suffers, all suffer together; if one member is honoured, all rejoice together" (1 Cor. 12:26). Your presence here reminds us of our common calling to extend hospitality as we seek to embody the unity Christ wills.

Let us greet the people around us and welcome each other to this place of worship.

When volunteers from different traditions gather

Blessed is our God always, now and ever and to the ages of ages. *Amen.*

We have come together from different congregations to work as one community united through our faith in Christ. "There is one body and one spirit, just as you were called to one hope that belongs to your call; one Lord, one faith, one baptism, one God and father of us all, who is above all and through all and in all" (Eph. 4: 4-5). Our labour is a witness to the conviction that Christian service is an essential mark of the church. We rejoice in this opportunity to be together, to work together and to pray together. May our ministry today be a blessing to all whom we serve.

Let us greet the people around us and pray for the fruitfulness of our shared ministry.

At congregational gatherings to which clergy from other traditions have been invited

Blessed is our God always, now and ever and to the ages of ages. *Amen.*

On behalf of the community gathered here today, we welcome you, our ecumenical guests who are our brothers and sisters in Christ. Thank you for joining us on this occasion. Your presence is a reminder of the real though incomplete unity that we share through our baptism, and of our common calling to reconciliation.

The names and titles of guests, their position and church affiliation may be mentioned at this time. The ecumenical guests may be invited to stand and face the assembly.

We pray for the healing of divisions among our churches, and look forward in hope to a time when we conform fully to Christ's prayer "that they may all be one" (John 17:21).

The apostle Paul urges us to "Welcome one another, therefore, as Christ has welcomed you, for the glory of God" (Rom. 15:7 RSV).

In this spirit, let us greet the people around us and welcome each other to this gathering.

When religious leaders are welcomed to a denominational event

Blessed is our God always, now and ever and to the ages of ages. *Amen.*

On behalf of this gathered community, we recognize and welcome the ecumenical guests who have been invited to share with us the experience of this day. These friends in Christ are a visible reminder that our unity is both a gift and a calling. We are grateful for your presence, we welcome your observations and we seek your prayers as we do the work of Christ in this place.

In the words of the apostle Paul, "Welcome one
another, therefore, as Christ has welcomed you
for the glory of God" (Rom. 15:7 RSV)

Let us greet the people around us and welcome each
other to this gathering.

When official representatives are welcomed at an ecumenical setting, such as a retreat centre

Blessed is our God always, now and ever and to the
ages of ages. *Amen.*

The scriptures urge us to "practise hospitality
ungrudgingly to one another. As each has
received a gift, employ it for one another, as good
stewards of God's varied grace" (1 Pet. 4: 9-10).
In the spirit of this counsel, we welcome you and
give thanks to God for the spiritual gifts you
bring. Your presence here is a reminder of our
common calling to unity through our Lord Jesus
Christ. We pray that in this time together, heart
will speak to heart for the glory of God.

And so we pray in the words our Saviour taught us:
Our Father...

Let us now greet the people around us and welcome
each other to this place.

When hospitality is offered at an ecumenical gathering, such as an assembly of a council of churches

When Christians come together in ecumenical
assembly, they invite God to bless the intentions of their
gathering in keeping with the prayer of our Lord "that
they may all be one" (John 17:21 RSV). The following
prayers from the Vancouver worship book of the World
Council of Churches[23] are examples of ways that Christians may pray together on such occasions.

Prayer of the Holy Spirit

Holy Spirit, Creator,
at the beginning you hovered over the waters;
you breathe life into all creatures;
without you every living creature dies and returns to
nothingness,

Come into us, Holy Spirit.

Holy Spirit, Comforter,
by you we are born again as children of God;
you make us living temples of your presence,
you pray within us with prayers too deep for words,

Come into us, Holy Spirit.

Holy Spirit, Lord and Giver of Life
you are light, you bring us light;
you are goodness and the source of all goodness,

Come into us, Holy Spirit.

Holy Spirit, Breath of life,
you sanctify and breathe life into the whole body of the
church;
you dwell in each one of its members,
and will one day give new life to our mortal bodies,

Come into us, Holy Spirit.

Prayer for Discipleship

O Lord our God, we thank you for
the many people throughout the ages
who have followed your way of life joyfully:
for the many saints and martyrs, men and women,
who have offered up their very lives,

so that your life abundant may become manifest
and your kingdom may advance.

For your love and faithfulness
we will at all times praise your name.

O Lord, we thank you for those
who chose the way of your Son
our brother Jesus Christ.
In the midst of trial, they held out hope;
in the midst of hatred, they kindled love;
in the midst of persecutions they witnessed to your
power;
in the midst of despair they clung to your promise.

For your love and faithfulness
we will at all times praise your name.

O Lord, we thank you for the truth they learned and
passed on to us:
that it is by giving that we shall receive;
it is by becoming weak that we shall be strong;
it is by loving others that we shall be loved;
it is by offering ourselves that the kingdom will unfold;
it is by dying that we shall inherit life everlasting.
Lord, give us courage to follow your way of life.

For your love and faithfulness
we will at all times praise your name.

Prayer for Peace and Unity

Dear friends, let us love one another, because love
comes from God.
Whoever loves is a child of God and knows God.

Jesus Christ, the life of the world, and of all creation,
Forgive our separation and grant us peace and unity.

The peace that Christ gives is to guide you
in the decisions you make;
for it is to this peace
that God has called you together in the one body.

Jesus Christ, the life of the world, and of all creation,
Forgive our separation and grant us peace and unity.

With his own body he broke down the wall that separated them.
By his death on the cross Christ destroyed their enmity.
By means of the cross he united
both races into one body.
In union with him you too are being built
together with all others
into a place where God lives through his Spirit.

Jesus Christ, the life of the world, and of all creation,
Forgive our separation and grant us peace and unity.

Do your best to preserve the unity which the Spirit gives
by means of the peace that binds you together.
There is one body, one spirit,
just as there is one hope to which God has called you.

Jesus Christ, the life of the world, and of all creation,
Forgive our separation and grant us peace and unity.

There is one Lord, one faith, one baptism;
there is one God who is Lord of all,
who works through all and in all. *Amen.*

NOTES

[1] Members of the working group noted that some traditions use words other than eucharist, such as the Lord's supper or holy communion, when they refer to this holy meal. Although the text is consistent in using the term "eucharist", the group recognizes and honours these other terms and traditions.

[2] R.E. Meagher, "Strangers at the Gate. Ancient Rites of Hospitality", *Parabola*, 2, 1977, pp.10-15 esp. p. 13.

[3] The unique story of the encounter between Sisera and Jael in Judges 4:17-21 is a striking example of the violation of several expectations in a guest-host relationship and of the fatal consequences; see V.H. Matthews, "Hospitality and Hostility in Judges 4", *Biblical Theology Review*, 21, 1991, pp.13-21.

[4] Unless otherwise noted, the scripture quotations contained herein are from the New Revised Standard Version Bible: © 1993 and 1989 by the Division of Christian Education of the National Council of the Churches of Christ in the USA. Used by permission. All rights reserved.

[5] B.J. Malina, "Hospitality", in J.J. Pilch and B.J. Malina eds, *The Handbook of Biblical Social Values*, Peabody MA, Hendrickson, 1998, pp.115-16.

[6] Conflicts over honour, patronage and the equality of participants appear in the symposium traditions which shaped ancient meal celebrations generally, see D.E. Smith, *From Symposium to Eucharist. The Banquet in the Early Christian World*, Minneapolis, Fortress, 2003, pp.11-12,56-58,82-83.

[7] Smith, *Symposium*, pp.51-55. Smith suggests that the rules for praying and prophesying in good order so that the Christian assembly is built up from 1 Corinthians 14 also belong to the context of rules for appropriate speech during the symposium part of a banquet (pp.206-207).

[8] In 1 Corinthians 9:19-23 and 10:32-11:1, he recommends a flexibility in adapting one's behaviour to those among whom one finds oneself in order to serve the gospel, a principle repeated in Romans 14:20-21.

[9] See Dale Martin, *The Corinthian Body*, New Haven CN, Yale, 1995.

[10] Smith, *Symposium*, pp.16-17,44-45.

[11] NRSV: "... do you with your acts of favouritism really believe in our glorious Lord Jesus Christ?"

[12] David B. Gowler, *Host, Guest, Enemy, and Friend: Portraits of the Pharisees in Luke and Acts*, New York, Peter Lang, 1991.

[13] Routine protocol (Smith, *Symposium*, p.27).

[14] Greek *hoti* clause is ambiguous; a causal use of the particle would suggest that her love is antecedent to the forgiveness (see Fitzmyer, *Luke I-IX*). NRSV translation assumes that the phrase conforms to the application of Jesus' parable of the two debtors (vv.41-43) as the final phrase in v.47b does.

[15] F. Bovon, *Luke I*, p.298, observes that sin and prejudice in society is overcome not by law but by encounter.

[16] Two terms have been used in Western theology: "circumincession"(from Latin *incedere*: to enter) denotes the movement towards and into the Other Persons; "circuminsession" (from Latin *insedere*: to sit) denotes the resulting indwelling.

[17] This is an ancient Christian affirmation still frequently expressed in the daily liturgical life of the Orthodox church.

[18] St Maximos the Confessor, *Mystagogia*, 24.

[19] St Maximos the Confessor, cited in *Patrum Spirituale* (Spiritual Meadow) by John Moschus and Sophronius, PG 87, 2925.

[20] St Gregory of Sinai, cited in Archbishop Paul of Finland, *The Faith We Hold,* Crestwood NY, St Vladimir's Seminary Press, 1980, p. 96.

[21] St Gregory of Nyssa, *On the Song of Songs,* 2.

[22] St Isaac the Syrian, *Concerning the Distinction of Virtues,* 91.

[23] *Jesus Christ, the Life of the World. A Worship Book for the Sixth Assembly of the World Council of Churches*, WCC, 1983, pp.10, 49 and 64. The first prayer is by the Taizé Community.

DATE DUE

HIGHSMITH #45230

Printed
in USA